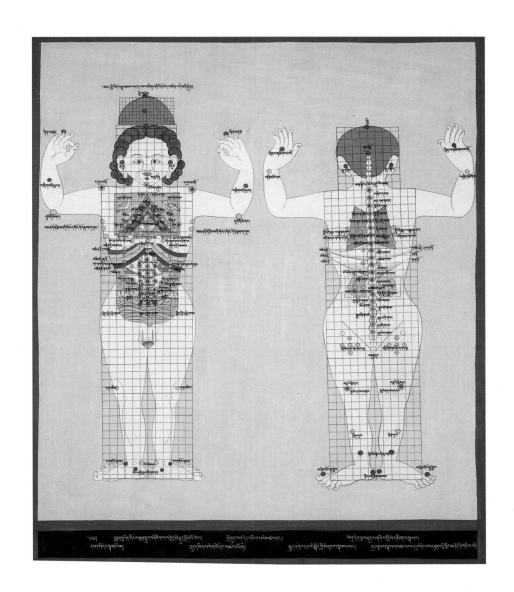

THE TIBETAN ART OF HEALING

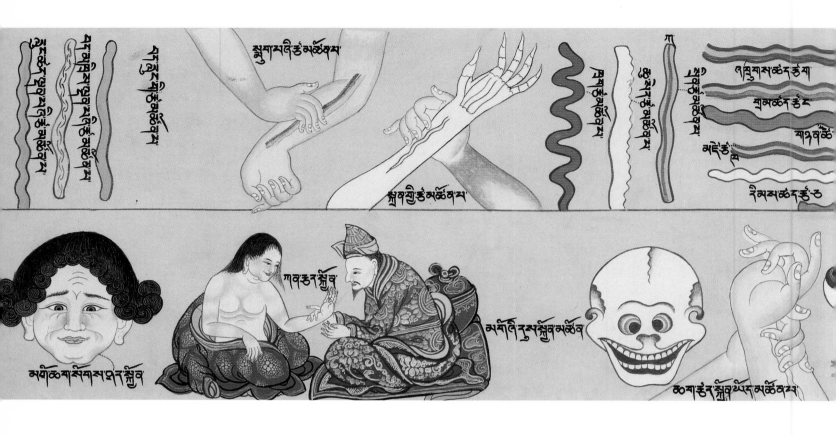

Ian A. Baker | Paintings by Romio Shesthra | Preface by Deepak Chopra

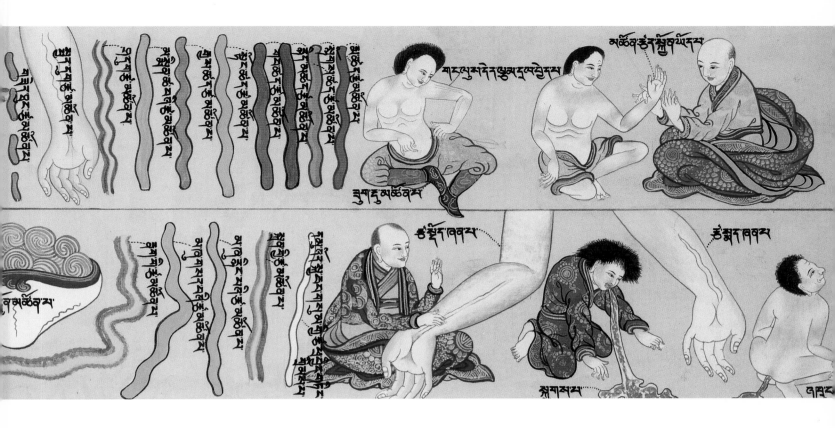

THE TIBETAN ART OF HEALING

with over 250 illustrations in colour

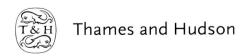

Thames and Hudson

This book is dedicated to the memory of Ian Middleton

The treatments and remedies illustrated in this book represent the state of medical knowledge and practices in Tibet at the end of the seventeenth century. The information recorded is not intended as a substitute for the recommendations of a health-care professional.

The publishers would like to thank The Academy of Everything is Possible for its support throughout.

The paintings reproduced in this book were specially photographed by Roy Hewson.

© 1997 Thames and Hudson Ltd, London
Paintings © 1997 Romio Shrestha

British Library Cataloguing-in-Publication Data
A catalogue record for this book is available from the British Library

ISBN 0-500-27996-9

Printed and bound in Singapore

PAGE 1: Diagram showing moxibustion points (indicated in red and black) and points for minor surgery (in yellow); see pp. 138–41.

PAGE 2-3: Detail of a thangka providing guidance on the diagnosis of various illnesses by examination of the pulses; see pp. 98–105.

PAGE 5: The four Tantras when combined resemble a Garuda, a hawk-like demi-god credited with powers of healing.

PAGE 6: Thangka devoted to human embryology, showing progressive stages of development from conception to birth; see pp. 40–43.

CONTENTS

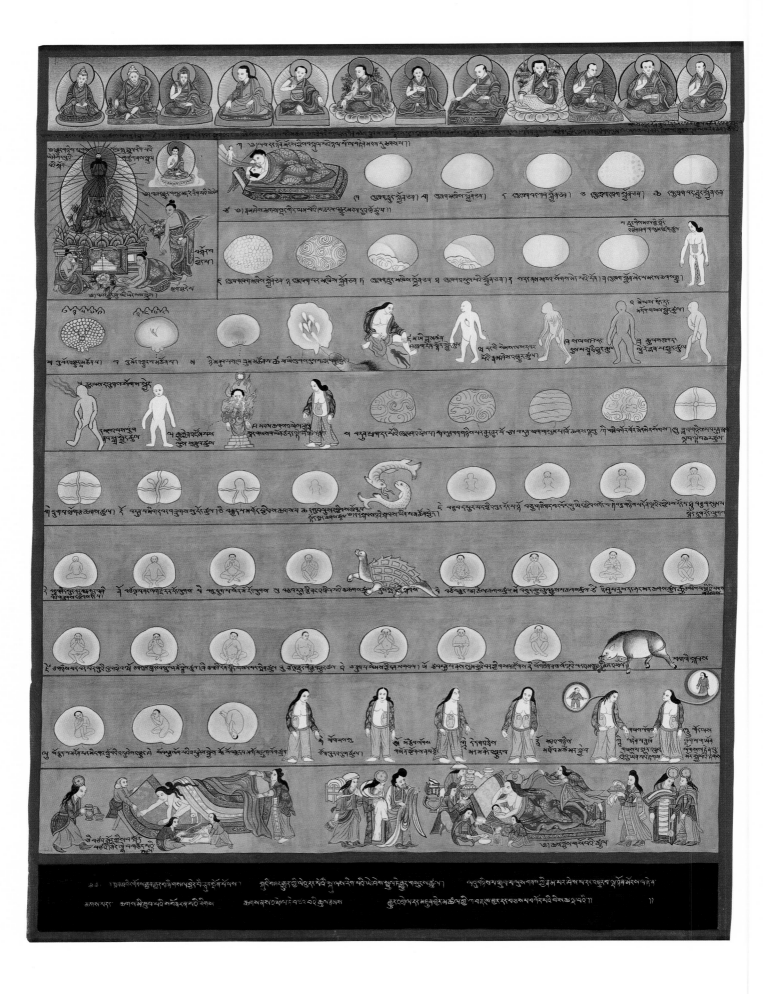

THE DALAI LAMA

Tibetan medicine is one of the greatest legacies of Tibetan Buddhist civilization. It is a system that can contribute substantially to maintaining a healthy mind and a healthy body. Like the traditional Indian and Chinese systems, Tibetan medicine views health as a question of balance. A variety of circumstances such as diet, lifestyle, seasonal and mental conditions can disturb this natural balance, which gives rise to different kinds of disorders.

As living beings we all wish to achieve happiness and avoid suffering. Our desire for health, for complete physical and mental well-being, is an expression of this, for everyone wants to be well and no one wishes to be sick. Consequently, health is not a matter of merely personal interest, but a universal concern for which we all share some responsibility. This is why the ideal physician is one who combines sound medical understanding with a strong realization of wisdom and compassion.

Tibetan medicine is deeply influenced by Buddhist practice and theory which stresses the indivisible interdependence of mind, body and vitality. As an integrated system of health care Tibetan medicine has served the Tibetan people well for many centuries and I believe can still provide much benefit to humanity at large. The difficulty we face in bringing this about is one of communication, for, like other scientific systems, Tibetan medicine must be understood in its own terms, as well as in the context of objective investigation.

I am confident that this book, which reproduces paintings from the Buddhist medical Tantras that were traditionally made as study aids for Tibetan doctors, will be of immense benefit for serious students of Tibetan medicine as well as providing an opportunity for general readers to appreciate this valuable but sometimes overlooked aspect of the Tibetan cultural heritage.

Preface: The Art of Healing

by Deepak Chopra

Many people, including physicians, have become disillusioned by the prevailing materialistic interpretation of illness and health. The revolution in health care emerging now in the West is based largely on the insights of ancient India and Tibet, where healing and spirituality were intimately linked. In the traditional Ayurvedic and Tibetan approach to medicine the body is more than a mere life-support system: it is seen as a vehicle for realizing perfect health in body, mind and spirit – a bridge to our highest potential.

At the heart of the Tibetan medical tradition is the recognition that the physical world, including our bodies, is largely a product of our individual perception, and that it is the mind that directs the body towards sickness or health. The Tibetan-Ayurvedic model of disease allows us to see how our bodies often express inner, even subconscious, psychological states. The physician's role within this system is to guide the patient towards greater self-awareness, beyond the self-imposed limitations that foster disease. Ultimately, true healing begins when we discover within ourselves that place where we are linked with the larger forces of the universe. Although each person may seem separate and independent, all of us are connected to patterns of intelligence that govern the whole cosmos. Our bodies are part of a universal body, our minds an aspect of a universal mind.

When harmony prevails between the elements of human physiology and the forces of the macrocosm, nature's intelligence flows spontaneously through the cells of the body. Whether or not the physician resorts to the use of medications or external therapies, the patient is directed towards health-producing behaviour that restores dynamic equilibrium to body and mind, so leading to physical, emotional and spiritual well-being. Health then becomes a heightened state of vitality, creativity, peace and joy where we transcend the individual ego.

In my book *Quantum Healing* I demonstrated how consciousness creates reality and expectation decisively influences the result. Awareness, attention and intention should be as much a part of health care as drugs, radiation and surgery because, ultimately, one's state of consciousness is the most important element in the healing process. In Buddhist terms the transformation of mind and body begins with the experience of Sunyata – the pure, immeasurable potential of all that ever was, is or will be. The paintings presented in this book guide us vibrantly and directly into this world of limitless possibility.

Art in India and Tibet has always had the goal of reminding us of a higher reality, of our own inner potential. The paintings from the Buddhist medical Tantras are no exception. They are vivid tools for exploring the mind's role in creating illness and health, as well as for discovering the place within us where the body's innate intelligence mirrors the wisdom of the Cosmos.

The Tibetan medical thangkas featured in this book are the work of an exceptionally gifted artist who was recognized at the age of five as the reincarnation of a revered painter from Tibet. Romio's art is celestial. His luminous and extraordinary paintings work on multiple levels to evoke the healing response from

within. The paintings reveal the vast variety of diseases that human beings are subject to, as well as the intricacies of an ancient and profound system of healing. In them are depicted the attitudes and behaviour that lead to suffering as well as those which lead to health, so introducing us to new ways of understanding the link between mind and body. They also introduce in graphic detail the diagnostic and therapeutic procedures of Tibetan medicine, including pulse divination, dietary modification, yogic exercises, meditation and massage. The paintings impart knowledge in a spontaneous and effortless manner. As we contemplate these timeless images, a shift in consciousness occurs. The conceptual mind is stilled, and a new vision of health and healing begins to unfold.

Such shifts in consciousness bring transformation within the body. It is my experience that we metabolize our sensory experiences into physiological responses. There is an ancient Buddhist expression: 'If you want to know what your experiences were like in the past, examine your body now. If you want to know what your body will be like in the future, look at your experience now.'

Religious art in the Tibetan tradition represents symbolically the dynamic interplay of macro- and microcosm. The mere sight of such art can invoke within our physiology a memory of wholeness. The Sanskrit word *Smriti* refers to the subtle memory embedded within every cell of our body. The word 'healing' originates from 'holy', which in turn derives from the word 'whole'. When the memory of wholeness is restored, healing takes place within our mind and body. The *Smriti*, or memory, of that original wholeness is always present on a cellular level, but is overshadowed by our habitual inattention and our preoccupation with trivial and mundane affairs.

When we meditate on a painting that has within it the memory of wholeness, our attention shifts from the superficial turbulent activity of the world to a transcendental reality: a realm of peace, harmony, laughter and joy. Restoring these qualities to our consciousness once again allows the flow of nature's intelligence throughout the body. The great achievement of Tibetan Buddhist art, and the Tibetan medical thangkas in particular, is its revelation of the human organism as a vehicle of transcendance and spiritual liberation. It is my great pleasure to introduce these paintings, which bring a visual dimension to the work that I have been introducing in my own books, seminars and clinical practice.

The physical body is a by-product of the more subtle aspects of our existence. By influencing these subtle levels we begin to transform our sense of who and what we are. These paintings from the Tibetan medical tantras take us on a journey not just through an exotic world of disease and healing, but they can affect us on the level of the subtle body – the inner reservoir of feelings, emotions, desires and memories. They may also act on the causal body, the locus of the very software of our souls.

The art of healing is achieved when all our actions are inspired by a higher reality in which our individual identity is inseparable from the creative forces of the Cosmos. It is my profound belief that great art can initiate the healing response within us, and urge us beyond all limited self-identifications, beyond time and boundaries. This is the liberated state of the Buddhas, the awakened ones, towards which these paintings guide us. May these images of human potential help beings everywhere to rediscover the state of perfect health and spiritual well-being!

Introduction: The Tibetan medical tradition

The unique quality of Tibetan medicine lies not only in its clear commitment to healing the human body of illness and disease, but, equally, in its revelation of a path in which body, mind and spirit can be liberated from the sufferings of conditioned existence. According to Tibetan tradition, the Buddha, emanating as the 'Master of Remedies', established the basis of Tibetan medicine thousands of years ago in the form of the Gyushi, or Four Medical Tantras. In the seventeenth century Sangye Gyamtso, regent to the Fifth Dalai Lama, wrote a commentary to the Gyushi called the Blue Beryl which he then had illustrated with a series of extraordinary paintings offering insights into the Tibetan Buddhist approach to health, healing and spirituality.

The majority of the original paintings commissioned by Sangye Gyamtso in 1687 and kept at the Chagpori Medical College in Lhasa were destroyed by the Chinese in 1959 in the course of the 'liberation' of Tibet. Two later editions completed in 1923, during the period of the Thirteenth Dalai Lama, survive in Lhasa at the School of Medicine and Astrology (Mentsekhang) and at the Dalai Lama's former summer palace. A third set of medical paintings dating to the same period was recently discovered in the archives of the Buryiat Historical Museum in Ulan-Ude, southern Siberia.

An extraordinary modern edition of the historic Tibetan medical paintings has been created by the Nepalese artist Romio Shrestha. Masterfully painted on a gold background, the paintings that emerged from Shrestha's school of Tibetan thangka painting are based upon the medical paintings in Lhasa as well as upon those preserved in Ulan-Ude. Each edition faithfully reproduces Sangye Gyamtso's lost originals with minor variations in keeping with the artistic licence allowed in non-iconographical Buddhist art. The set of scroll paintings, each approximately 62 cm (25 in.) wide,

Mandala of the Medicine Buddha

opposite

The first thangka in the series of paintings illuminating Sangye Gyamtso's commentary to the Tibetan medical Tantras reveals the celestial realm of the Medicine Buddha, Bhaishajyaguru. Emanating from a palace adorned with healing jewels and surrounded by forests of fragrant herbs and medicinal plants, the Medicine Buddha is the primordial image of the divine healer. The sky-blue light radiating from his body disperses the darkness of afflictive emotions and all related physical disorders. Surrounded by a retinue of gods, sages and naked ascetics (described as sleeping at night under blankets of leaves and by day wearing only the bark of trees), the Medicine Buddha – the supreme benefactor known as the King of Aquamarine Light – expounded the quintessence of healing and longevity in a discourse entitled the 'Tantra of Secret Instructions on the Eight Branches of the Essence of Immortality', more commonly referred to as the Gyushi, or Four Medical Tantras.

produced by Shrestha has been exhibited in Europe and the United States, bringing attention to what has until now remained a relatively unknown approach to healing and spiritual development.

As a visual supplement to the Buddhist medical Tantras, the seventy-nine thangkas featured in the Nepalese edition include nearly eight thousand distinct images. Tibetan doctors, indeed, devote several years' study to the paintings and the texts they illuminate. Nonetheless, as Sangye Gyamtso described his work in the late seventeenth century, this series of 'paintings without any equivalent in the past was established in order that the content [of the medical Tantras] could be perceived by everybody, from the scholar to the child, as clearly as one would see a myrobalan plant held in the palm of one's hand.' The inspiration behind Romio Shrestha's work was similarly based on making the essence of the Buddhist system of healing accessible to a wider audience. 'I have always felt', Shrestha said, 'that art can convey truths that academic treatises only touch upon. The images within these paintings are keys to understanding the healing response within our own bodies and minds. They are potent examples of the Tibetan Buddhist concept of "Liberation through sight".'

Discourses of the Medicine Buddha

below right

'The Supreme Healer, the King of Aquamarine Light entered into meditative absorption, with rays of multi-coloured light radiating from his heart in all ten directions, dissolving the mental defilements of all animate beings and pacifying ailments which arise from ignorance. Then drawing the light rays back to his heart, the magical form of the Buddha Rigpa Yeshe emanated from his mind. Appearing in the sky before him, he beseeched the Sovereign Healer, "O Master. As we desire to obtain this bounty for the sake of ourselves and others, how may we learn the oral teachings on the science of healing?"'

The Ambrosia Heart Tantra

The Buddhist path to health and liberation

Some 2,500 years ago, the Buddha Sakyamuni, distressed at the prospect of old age, sickness and death, discovered a path in which the suffering that attends human existence could be alleviated, and its root cause – a sense of identity narrowly defined by the physical body and self-limiting thoughts and emotions – be transformed into radiant equanimity. Traditionally, the Buddha is considered the supreme healer, while our erroneous conceptions of reality are seen as the root of all disease and discontent. A Buddhist Sutra states:

'Noble one, think of yourself as someone who is sick,
Of the Dharma as the remedy,
Of your spiritual friend as a skilful doctor
And of diligent practice as the way to recover.'

The earliest Buddhist scriptures describe suffering as arising
from our habitual attempts to secure ourselves within an ever-
shifting universe. Excessive attachment, the Buddha taught,
particularly to the body, gives rise to suffering, as impermanence
and change are central to all life: through meditation identification
with ego gradually diminishes and insight develops into the
evanescent nature of all existence. Correct understanding leads
to Nirvana – the cessation of all suffering.

In the second century BC, three hundred years after the
passing of Sakyamuni Buddha, a set of scriptures called
Prajnaparamita, or Perfection of Wisdom, initiated new
developments in Buddhist thought and practice. In the
Mahayana, or Greater Vehicle, as the new movement
came to be known, the Buddhist aspiration was
no longer to secure personal salvation, but to strive
for the benefit of all sentient beings. Compassion
was revealed as the essential energy animating all
existence, obscured only by false conceptions of
the self. Only after renouncing all self-clinging,
the Mahayana texts declared, could the nature
of reality be revealed. The Bodhisattva vow
of working for the benefit of all beings
established compassionate activity and
the alleviation of human suffering as

above

In Tibetan Buddhism the more
familiar tradition associated with
celibate monasticism is paralleled
by an order of free-roaming Tantric
yogins whose quest for truth is
based not on renunciation but on
the premise of Primordial Purity
(*Kadag*) as the source of all thought
and appearance.

the fundamental Buddhist ideals. It was during this period that
the study of medicine was introduced as part of the curriculum in
monastic institutions, healing the sick being a practical method of
living out the virtue of selfless service, as well as a skilful means
of propagating the doctrine.

However, it was in the revelation of the Buddhist Tantras – the
esoteric texts and secret practices that ensure liberation in a single
lifetime – that the Buddhist art of healing was to attain its full
development. The body was no longer conceived of as an obstacle
or hindrance on the path towards enlightenment; instead it was
recognized as the primary vehicle. As stated in the Tantras, 'This
body is the very body of the Buddhas, more precious than a wish-
fulfilling gem.' In the Buddhist Tantras the body was revealed as
a reservoir of bliss, an abode of dormant energies that, properly
cultivated, unfold into a body of light.

The essential practices of Tantra are based on an inner alchemy
in which the base constituents of the body/mind are purified and
transformed. Perceiving the material world, including the human
body, as the luminous expression of universal intelligence, the
practitioner of Tantra views the body's inner mandala of winds,
channels and subtle essences as the natural radiance of wisdom
and compassion. As the Tibetan sage Longchenpa has proclaimed,

'Since practitioners of Tantra recognize all phenomena as inherently pure, they can transform everything into a means of liberation.'

From the eighth century on, the esoteric Tantric path was brought from India to Tibet, and disseminated there by the great sage Padmasambhava. For centuries following his departure, Tibetans travelled across the Himalayas in search of Buddhist teachings to penetrate the veils obscuring our innermost nature, which in Buddhist thought lies beyond both sickness and health. The quest for healing, for wholeness, is the perennial dream of the human species, and nowhere was it elucidated with greater subtlety and depth than in the Buddhist Tantras. In the words of the great Tantric *siddha* Saraha, 'Although scholars can expound the sacred texts, they do not recognize the great wisdom dwelling within the body.' Transforming our attitudes about the world around us, about our bodies and the nature of consciousness itself, the Buddhist art of healing presents a new vision of human potential, a wisdom emerging not from some transcendental heaven, but from the subtle essences concealed in the innermost recesses of our bodies and minds.

Sage-physicians

below

The lineage of the Buddhist medical Tantras includes ancient Indian as well as Tibetan sages renowned for their supernormal powers of healing and cognition.

below

The Tibetan practice of pulse diagnosis has its origins in Chinese medicine, in which it has been used for over 2,000 years. Developing extraordinary levels of sensitivity, the accomplished physician attunes the tips of his fingers to neural and circulatory patterns within the patient's body, which yield detailed information about the patient's state of health.

Tibetan medicine: history and origins

The Tibetan medical tradition traces its origins to the revelations of the Buddha in his manifestation as Bhaishajyaguru, or Master of Remedies – the propounder of the Four Medical Tantras which constitute the basis of the Tibetan medical paintings. Dr Yeshi Donden, former personal physician to the present Dalai Lama, has explained that 'As Buddha represents the awakened intelligence of all beings, he is considered the primordial source of all branches of healing.'

Historically, the emergence of a sophisticated medical system in Tibet dates to the reign of the seventh-century King Songtsen Gampo. Eager to develop cultural exchanges with neighbouring countries, the monarch invited physicians from India, China and Iran to the Tibetan court. According to the Tibetan chronicles, it was at this earliest of medical conferences that treatises and texts representing the different medical traditions were translated into the newly formulated Tibetan language. In the century following, the translation of medical works continued under the patronage

ཞེས་སློར་བ

of King Trisongdetsen, who, following the precedent set by his predecessor, invited to Tibet physicians from Persia, India, Kashmir, Nepal, China and Turkic regions of Central Asia. It was during this period that the Four Tantras which are attributed to Bhaishajyaguru are said to have been translated from the original Sanskrit and hidden in a pillar of Samye monastery, where they remained concealed until the eleventh century.

In the twelfth century, a descendant of Yuthok Yonten Gonpo, court physician to Trisongdetsen, was credited with the authorship of a revised version of the Four Tantras which incorporated indigenous Tibetan traditions of shamanic healing, as well as Tantric and alchemical treatises pertaining to mystical physiology and the attainment of longevity. So effective did Tibetan medicine become that in the thirteenth century, while the country was under Mongol rule, Tibetan monk-physicians succeeded in converting the court of Kublai Khan to Buddhism through what were perceived as miraculous displays of healing and divination.

Several centuries later, during the period of the Fifth Dalai Lama, Tibet's first hospital and medical college were established on a hill site adjacent to the Potala Palace in Lhasa. Dating from 1696, the

Healing herbs

above
....
For centuries many practical aspects of medicine were exchanged between China, India and Tibet. Supplies of hemp, sandalwood, cardamom, camphor, datura (thorn apple) and cinnamon were imported from India, while rhubarb, sarsaparilla, angelica, licorice, ginseng, mugwort and tea were brought from China. Some of the most precious medicinal substances such as cordyceps and musk were found primarily in Tibet.

Foundations of healing

opposite

This thangka begins with procedures and substances integral to the attainment of health and longevity. Foods with medicinal properties are pictured in the second panel. The third panel illustrates the qualities of a reliable physician and an attentive nurse. The subsequent panels indicate patients who are worthy or capable of being cured, as well as those who are not. The latter include those who revel in killing, those who reject the advice of their doctors, those who indulge in excessive emotionalism, who destroy sacred Buddha images, or who are on the brink of death. The third to last panel depicts approaches a doctor must take in treating disease. At times he must proceed gradually as if ascending a ladder or, in the case of complex symptoms, as if settling a dispute between warring parties. The treatment of serious diseases is likened to the heavy load carried by a hybrid cow, and that of lesser diseases to a lighter load carried by a sheep. The lower two panels illustrate various diagnostic tests and decoctions.

King of medicines

below

The astringent fruits of the various types of arura, or chebulic myrobalan, are considered great panaceas.

Chagpori Medical College enriched its curriculum with monastic rites focusing on the invocation of healing deities, on rituals associated with longevity and on the consecration of compounded medicines. In order to clarify the contents of the Four Tantras, the seminal texts in the study of Tibetan medicine, the Dalai Lama's regent, Sangye Gyamtso, composed his erudite commentary called the Vaidurya Ngonpo, or Blue Beryl. In order to elucidate its contents he commissioned the original series of paintings upon which the modern versions reproduced in the present book are based.

In 1916, during the period of the Thirteenth Dalai Lama, a second medical college, called Mentsekhang, was founded in Lhasa at the initiative of a revered physician named Khenrab Norbu. Two additional sets of medical paintings were produced in the years following to be employed in the training of a new generation of Tibetan doctors.

Although the Chagpori Medical College was destroyed in 1959, along with its library and the original paintings commissioned by Sangye Gyamtso nearly three hundred years earlier, the more secular Mentsekhang was spared and still operates in Lhasa, albeit within the confines of Chinese Communist ideology – a concession made in recognition of the therapeutic efficacy of traditional Tibetan medicine. Chagpori has recently been re-established in the Indian hill town of Darjeeling under the directorship of a master physician named Trogawa Rinpoche, who sustains the vital link between Buddhist practice and the arts of healing.

Foundations of the Four Tantras

Covering the topics of physiology, pathology, diagnosis and cure, the Four Tantras (Gyushi) form the basis of the Tibetan medical system. Composed in the form of a dialogue between emanations of the Medicine Buddha, Bhaishajyaguru, the original manuscript of the Four Tantras is said to have been written on sheets of gold with ink made from lapis lazuli and placed in the custody of celestial nymphs. The revised version of the Four Tantras in use today, consisting of 5,900 verses, was compiled in the twelfth century and integrates medical knowledge gathered throughout Tibet, Asia and the Middle East.

Derived from the Indian medical system of Ayurveda, the threefold division of bodily energy based on the Five Elements (earth, water, fire, air and space) is central to all aspects of Tibetan medicine. Disturbances to these inner elements, caused by dietary factors or environmental stress, lead to illness and death. Healing modalities focus on restoring and maintaining a proper balance

The tree of physiology

opposite

The second thangka illustrating Sangye Gyamtso's commentary is composed as a tree with two trunks, one depicting the various branches of human physiology, and the other its pathological transformations. The upper panel illustrates the lineage of medical teaching, beginning with an emanation of the Medicine Buddha and including his fourfold retinue of gods, hermit sages, Hindu divinities and Buddhist masters.

The inner winds

below

Two of the five types of *loong*, or psycho-physical 'winds': the life-sustaining breath which circulates from the top of the head down to the diaphragm, and the ascending wind which controls speech and memory.

When the elements and psycho-physical constituents of the human body are properly regulated and balanced by appropriate diet and behaviour, vibrant health serves as the foundation for spiritual and material well-being, symbolized as the flowers of a wish-fulfilling tree. Pictured as a Buddha dissolving into light, the ultimate fruit is described as the obtaining of unsurpassed enlightenment, the liberation of the body's psycho-physical components in the blissful expanse of light.

Anatomical grids

right

Serving as a reference system and scale of measurement, grid patterns overlaid on anatomical drawings are a feature found only in Tibetan art, although the anthropometric units of measurement upon which they are based are analogous to those used in Chinese medicine. In the example illustrated the grid pattern provides a template which can be used by the physician to determine the precise locations from which pathogenic fluids can be extracted from the body.

between these three psycho-physical 'humours' (Wind, Bile and Phlegm) – a holistic process which takes into account personality, season, age, diet, behaviour and physical environment. Along with methods based on indigenous Tibetan shamanism and esoteric Tantric rites, the medical texts also describe techniques of pulse diagnosis, acupuncture and moxibustion, notably distinct from their Chinese or lesser-known Indian counterparts. Unique, however, to the Buddhist tradition is the ideal of liberation not only from physical ailments, but from the subtle afflictions of mind and emotion that obscure enlightened awareness. Through methods involving the transformation of winds, energies and subtle essences within the body, the same channels through which disease occurs are purified into vehicles of spiritual liberation.

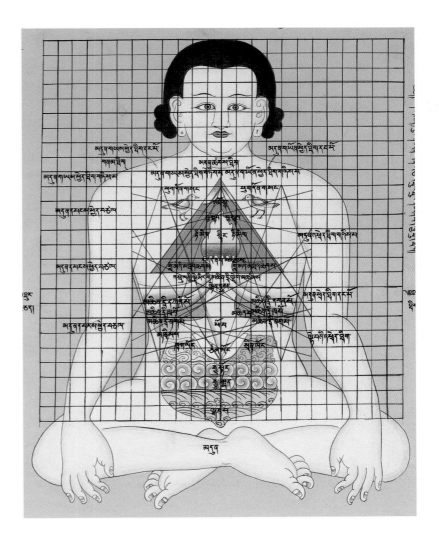

Transfiguration of the healer

opposite

In Tibetan medical tradition, the knowledge gained by physicians truly dedicated to the alleviation of human suffering results in qualities identical to those of the Buddha.

The body of elements

left

The psycho-physical energies represented by the five elements – earth, water, fire, air and space – circulate throughout the body. When purified through visualization and Tantric yogas, these same elements that cause disease become the basis of enlightenment.

Subduer of disease

below

A wrathful emanation of enlightened consciousness, the deity Dorje Tabring is invoked to subdue the demons and spirits believed to cause disease. The images of gods, demons and enlightened beings in the medical paintings encourage not superstitious belief, but the capacity to imagine ourselves unbounded by conventional perceptions.

The art of transformation

As a support for meditation, art in Tibetan Buddhism is based on the revelation of archetypal realities that are normally absent from conscious thought. Originally created as visual aids for aspiring healers, the Tibetan medical paintings became sources of inspiration not only for physicians, but also for patients and pilgrims who frequented the two Tibetan medical colleges, Mentsekhang and Chagpori. The thangkas reveal in condensed form the entire contents of the Four Tantras – from the opening mandala, the doorway into the world of healing and transformation, to the final images of the healer-physician absorbed into a sphere of rainbow light.

Although the content of the medical paintings draws on elements from classical Indo-Tibetan iconography, and the horizontal panels which illustrate the text of the Blue Beryl are derived from earlier Nepalese models, the composition of many of the thangkas is unique and without precedent. The 'unfolded trees' which serve to illustrate the various branches of Tibetan medical science, as well as the various thangkas in which the origin of poisons and the elixirs of longevity are depicted, are

The power to heal, the Tantras claim, comes only when the contents of books and medical treatises have been assimilated into one's very being. Then, like the rays of the sun, knowledge illuminates all experience, just as precious gold and turquoise concealed in a treasure chest will yield themselves to anyone who holds the key.

entirely original creations, while the appearance of Buddhas throughout the paintings reminds the viewer of a transcendental reality preceding the transient experiences of illness and pain.

The thangkas featured in this book were all painted on sized canvas with water-soluble pigments made from ground minerals and plants mixed with glue. Gold dust was used for the outlines of many of the figures, adding exceptional richness to the finished paintings. According to Romio Shrestha, the artists of his school follow the traditional practices involved in the creation of sacred art, visualizing themselves as the deities depicted and absorbing their spiritual energies before committing the images to canvas. The paintings thus become vibrant symbols of selfless creativity and the healing power of art. As Shrestha has described his work, 'The art of thangka painting is inspired by the universal human

overcome suffering and to gain happiness and longevity. In the Buddhist view, this goal only becomes possible when we work not for ourselves but for all beings.'

In Tibetan Buddhism the artist uses form and beauty, as well as images that we tend more often to suppress, to transform ordinary perception into healing awareness. Scenes depicting suffering and disease, cruelty and lust, as well as images of transcendental joy, reveal how events of everyday life, depending on our degree of openness and compassion, can become sources of either suffering or liberation. Portraying the entire spectrum of human experience, and restoring wholeness to our normally selective awareness, the medical paintings reveal how the essential ingredients for spiritual transformation exist within the very desires and aversions that define our contracted lives.

Qualities of the physician

above

As described in the Tibetan medical
Tantras, the accomplished physician
should be like an alert falcon in his
ability to distinguish between different
constitutional disorders. He should be
patient like a sheep in his observation
of fluctuating symptoms, and as
cautious as a fox in his prescribing
of remedies when diseases reach
maturity. In treating relapses and
complications, the doctor should be
as brave and decisive as a tiger.

The Tibetan physician

The training of a Tibetan doctor covers all aspects of the arts of
healing, from the identification and processing of medicinal plants
to the meditative empathy essential for successful diagnosis. After
fourteen years of preliminary education, a doctor's training consists
of five to twelve years of rigorous study, during which he develops
practical skills in the fields of pulse diagnosis, pharmacology,
acupuncture, moxibustion and methods for the purification and
empowerment of medicinal substances. In Tibetan medicine
a doctor's inner qualities are considered just as important as his
academic expertise. As K. Dhondrup wrote, 'Knowledge and skill
alone are not enough to become a good doctor. Love, kindness and
compassion toward patients and a sincere effort to share their
tension and distress is an equal – if not more – important and
essential quality of a doctor.'

For the Tibetan physician, the Buddhist ideals of wisdom and
compassion which are essential elements in his training further aid
him in attending to the physical, emotional and spiritual needs of

ষ্ণুন'ই'ষ্ণ্লব্ণ   ন্যাব'ষ্ণ্ৰ্ন্

his patients. Doctors therefore begin each day by visualizing
themselves in the form of the Medicine Buddha and recite texts
invoking his presence: 'As all sentient beings, infinite as space, are
encompassed by the compassion of the Master of Remedies, may
I too become their guide. . . . May I quickly attain the healing
powers of the Medicine Buddha, Bhaishajyaguru, and lead all
beings into his enlightened realm.'

Practised widely throughout Tibet, as well as in the Himalayan
regions of Ladakh, Nepal, Sikkim and Bhutan, the Tibetan art of
healing continues to be passed down through family lineages or,
more systematically, through the Tibetan medical college in
Lhasa or the Institute of Tibetan Medicine established in 1961
in Dharamsala (Himachal Pradesh), northern India – seat of the
Tibetan government-in-exile. Following the flight of the ethnic
population from Chinese-occupied Tibet, Tibetan medicine is
undergoing a process of continual development, including the
formulation of new remedies used in the treatment of cancer and
diseases of the immune system. As the Dalai Lama has stated,

The character of a nurse

above

As illustrated in the medical paintings, a sick person's nurse or companion should be competent, compassionate, pure in body, speech and mind, as well as knowledgable and intelligent, this last quality being symbolized by the books she carries on her back.

The healing nectar

opposite below

The contents of the medical Tantras should be cherished as a substance more precious than the milk of the mythical snow lion. By improperly guarding their essential precepts, or entrusting them to an unsuitable disciple, the nectar that alleviates human suffering is lost, like milk stored in a cracked container.

Tibetan medicine is an integrated system of health care that 'has served the Tibetan people well for many centuries and [which], I believe, can still provide much benefit to humanity at large. The difficulty we face in bringing this about is one of communication, for, like other scientific systems, Tibetan medicine must be understood in its own terms, as well as in the context of objective investigation.' Visits made by Tibetan doctors to Europe and the United States have led to new research in the fields of mind/body interaction, as well as to successful treatments of a variety of diseases resistant to more conventional therapy. Commenting on his meeting with Dr Yeshi Donden, one of Tibet's foremost medical practitioners, Dr Richard Selzer, professor of surgery at Yale University, noted that 'We have nothing like it in the West. It's a dimension of medicine that we have not yet realized.'

The Tibetan medical tradition, with its ancient roots in Buddhist philosophy and shamanic healing, is as valuable today as it was at the time of its inception. With sophisticated diagnostic techniques that are based not on the use of machines but on the physician's heightened sensitivity to the flow of internal energy and his knowledge of healing plants and techniques of potentization, Tibetan medicine provides not just a resource for overcoming transient illnesses and disease, but a fully integrated system for developing our latent psychic and spiritual capacities. Throughout the Tibetan medical system the goal is implicit: we heal the body to liberate the spirit and overcome conceptual structurings of reality. The Gyushi, the seminal text of all branches of Tibetan medicine,

states: 'O friends, know that he who wishes to remain free of illness and who seeks to cure others of disease should study the oral teaching of the science of healing. He who desires long life, wealth, happiness and spiritual knowledge should study these profound teachings . . . and strive to liberate all beings from the miseries of ignorance and disease.'

Liberating body and mind

right

Tibetan medicine is unique in that it expresses the enlightened teachings of the Medicine Buddha, Bhaishajyaguru. As Namkha Rinpoche explained, 'The Medicine Buddha is more than a healer of either the body or the mind. He is the supreme force of unobstructed compassion that illuminates the entire world – the healing energy of our innermost being.'

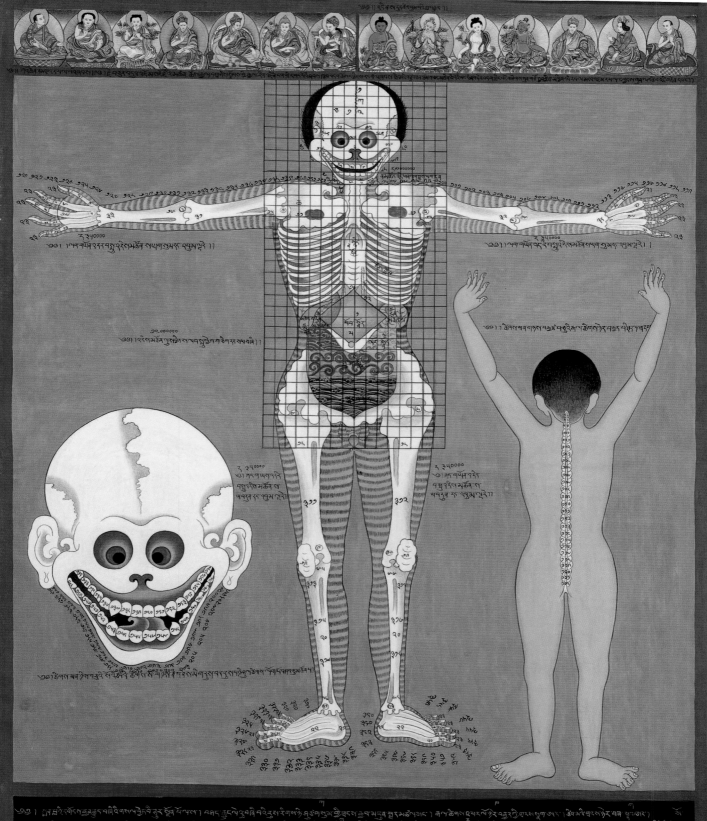

1 The body: vessel of transformation

Impermanent and subject to both pain and pleasure, our bodies are the central focus for our experience as human beings. Based on the insights of Tantric Buddhism, Tibetan medical tradition regards the body less as a potential vessel of disease than as the very means for overcoming the limited awareness at the root of all illness. Within our physical bodies, Tibetans claim, lie subtle energies that link us to all existence. Preoccupation with outer appearances, however, restricts our experience of this underlying reality, constraining us to a world filled with suffering and discontent.

In Tibetan medical philosophy, our self-limiting attitudes to the physical body are regarded as the cause of most physical and emotional distress. From the moment we are born our bodies are in a state of ceaseless transformation. Resistance to the body's innate cycles of decay and regeneration prevents us from ever penetrating the deeper mysteries that impermanence conceals. As one Tibetan physician noted, 'It is our very attachment to the body's physical form that obscures its essential nature. The Buddha himself declared: "Our body is precious. It is a vehicle of awakening." By clinging to it, however, we never see it for what it is.'

The paintings from the Blue Beryl contain thousands of images of the human body in varying states of sickness and health. Twenty-three thangkas of the original series are devoted to human anatomy, including the subtlemost energy channels that, in Tantric yoga, serve as the basis for recognizing our interconnectedness with the entire cosmos. The Tibetan medical paintings mirror these inner reflections, offering a potent source of insight and revelation. Contemplating the body in this way, we turn away from the ephemeral passions that largely characterize our lives and approach the true potential of human embodiment.

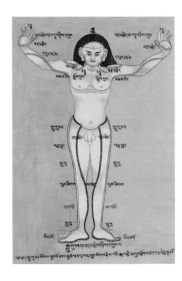

Vehicle of enlightenment

above

'The body is a mandala. If we look inside, it is an endless source of revelation . . . Without embodiment there is no foundation from which to gain enlightenment.'

Dr Tsampa Ngawang

Images of impermanence

opposite

In charnel grounds where Tibetans learned the rudiments of human anatomy, the transformations of the physical body were regarded as a means of developing detachment and awakening to a deeper reality. Contemplating the impermanence of all life revealed that death itself could be regarded as a transition to another state of existence, a doorway to liberation.

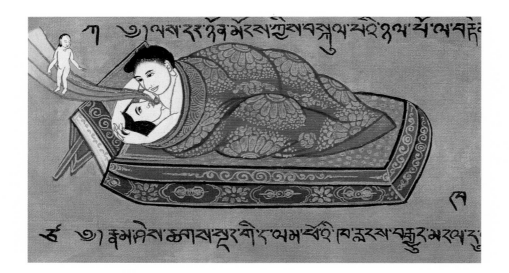

Conception

left

If a child is to be born male, its consciousness enters the mother's womb through the breath and semen of the father.

Male, female, hermaphrodite

opposite above

In addition to male and female genders, Tibetan medicine distinguishes a third sex that combines elements of both the others, as well as rare beings who are male the first half of the month and female in the second.

Auspicious birth

opposite, centre

According to the Blue Beryl, when birth proceeds correctly, 'the baby's head should emerge first . . . The umbilical cord should be wrapped around the upper body, the crying should be loud, and the mouth and tongue should suck strongly on the mother's breast.'

To possess a human body is considered by Tibetans to be a rare opportunity – far preferable even to being reborn as a god. For only in human life, Tibetans explain, is there the proper admixture of pleasure and pain that serves as a catalyst on the spiritual path. At the time of conception, the parents' passion and mingled essences combine to create a gateway through which the child's disembodied consciousness can once again seek birth – driven by the winds of karma and by the recurring desire for human incarnation.

According to Tibetan medical philosophy, all animate and inanimate phenomena are composed of the five primordial elements – earth, water, fire, air and space – symbolizing the dynamic, interpenetrating forces within all nature. As Dr Yeshi Donden explained, 'Without earth there would be no foundation. Without water things would not cohere. Without fire things could not ripen or mature. Without air things could not grow and increase, and without space there would be no opportunity or place for growth to occur.' In the context of human physiology, the earth element is associated with physical components such as bones, skin, nails and hair. Water refers to all bodily fluids and fire to the heat associated with metabolism and digestion. Air, or wind, is the vital energy responsible for all voluntary and involuntary bodily functions, while space is linked

Red and white essences

above

The human embryo forms within the mother's womb from the conjunction of the white element of the father's semen and the red element of the mother's ovum, symbolized as uterine blood. As the foetus develops, the earth element contributes to the formation of bones, muscles, skin and eyes, as well as to the sense of smell. Water forms the blood, lymph and bodily fluids, along with the sense of taste. Fire supplies bodily warmth, healthy complexion and sight. Air is responsible for respiration and the sense of touch. Hearing and the cavities and orifices of the body correspond to space, which contains the essence of the other four elements.

to consciousness. Imbalances in the body's elements, as well as between the body and the elements of the external environment, lead to physiological disturbances and disease. At death the body's constituent elements dissolve into each other – earth into water, water into fire, fire into air. As the air element dissolves into space, those proficient in meditation recognize the elements' subtle essences as all-pervading light.

Underlying unity

below

'The five primordial elements are the basis of all living organisms, and their imbalance the underlying cause of all disease. Likewise, all curative medications are compounded from the same five elements . . . Body, disease and remedies are connected in a single elemental essence.'

The Blue Beryl

Body of elements

right

In the context of the body's chakra system, the earth element provides solidity and is associated with the lower body and the perineum. The water element is linked to the genitals and seminal essences, fire to the region of the navel, air to the heart centre, and space to the region of the throat and head. This image also reveals the architectural basis of the Buddhist stupa – in essence, an abstract three-dimensional representation of the subtle body.

In Tibetan medical theory, the form and energy of the human body arise from the primordial elements of earth, water, fire, air and space. In human physiology, the air element corresponds to a bio-energetic force called *loong*, roughly translatable as Wind. The fire element corresponds to another bodily humour called *tripa*, or Bile. The earth and water elements refer to *beygen*, or Phlegm.

Derived from the ancient Indian medical system of *tridosha*, Wind, Bile and Phlegm are the biological manifestations of the five cosmic elements, corresponding to Vata, Pitta and Kapha in Indian Ayurveda. The harmonious functioning of these three bio-energetic

Characteristics of the three humours

above

The physical characteristics of human beings dominated by one or other of the humours: 'Those with a excess of Wind tend to frailty and insomnia . . . and are prone to singing, laughter, pugnacity and lust . . . Those with a predominance of Bile . . . are prone to hunger and thirst. . . . Those with the nature of Phlegm tend to be fat and fair-complexioned. They are heavy sleepers . . . yet have the qualities of lions, lead- bulls, elephants, celestial eagles and the Hindu god Brahma.'

Locations of the humours

below

Inscriptions on the leaves state that 'Phlegm is located primarily in the upper body, Bile in the trunk, and Wind in the lower regions. . . . Wind moves through the bones and other bodily structures.'

processes ensures health and well-being. If the humours become imbalanced through improper diet or behaviour or seasonal influences, deficiencies of particular elements predispose the body to disease. In the higher practices of Tantric Buddhism these same bodily constituents correspond to the rarefied essences, energies and channels of the subtle body. When purified through the yogic practice, the very qualities that cause disease bring realization of the enlightened state.

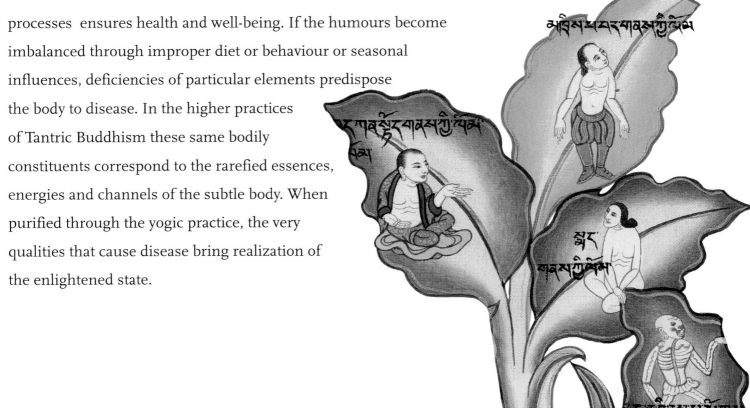

Models of mind and body

In the Tibetan medical system, the psycho-physical processes associated with Wind, Bile and Phlegm (*loong, tripa, beygen*) are the basis of all diagnosis and cure. Each human being is classified according to a naturally occurring predominance of one or more of the three humours, resulting in particular body types and dispositions. Although precise combinations of the humours can only be determined conclusively through urine and pulse diagnosis, self-observation alone can indicate which of the three humours is dominant within our own constitution, providing a mirror to look more deeply into our own and others' psycho-physical structure.

Symbolized by a bird representing movement as well as restlessness and desire, those with a predominance of Wind tend to be physically thin, to be sensitive to cold and susceptible to psychological conditions such as insomnia, asthma, tension and anxiety. Those whose predominant nature is *tripa*, or Bile, tend to be of medium height, and to sweat excessively. They are ambitious and intelligent, but prone to anger and impatience. They suffer headaches and sinus problems, as well as diseases of metabolism. When Phlegm dominates the constitution, individuals tend to be patient and stable, yet also lazy and overweight. They are particularly prone to chronic diseases of the sinus and digestive systems, as well as bronchial and kidney problems. The balance of the three humours changes throughout life, with Phlegm dominant in childhood and Wind in old age. The art of healing involves creating and maintaining a dynamic equilibrium between these three divisions of human physiology and the corresponding realms of thought, will and emotion.

Aspects of the three humours

opposite

A lower branch of the 'tree of physiology and pathological transformations' illustrates the five types of Wind, Bile and Phlegm which constitute the body's three humours. Linked to the central and peripheral nervous systems, the five types of Wind, as illustrated on the first five leaves on the lower half of the branch, govern the body's pulmonary and cardiovascular activity, speech, digestive processes, excretion, circulation and growth. The five types of Bile illustrated in the leaves following are associated with the gall bladder, small intestines, blood and lymph. Their actions include the regulation of body temperature and metabolism. Phlegm, which is structurally composed of water and earth and illustrated in the remaining five leaves, maintains fluid circulation and regulates the initial stages of digestion. As Dr Donden stated, 'When they are in a state of balance, the three humours and their fifteen subdivisions are instrumental in maintaining and improving health. The moment that they are disturbed, they become causes for disease.'

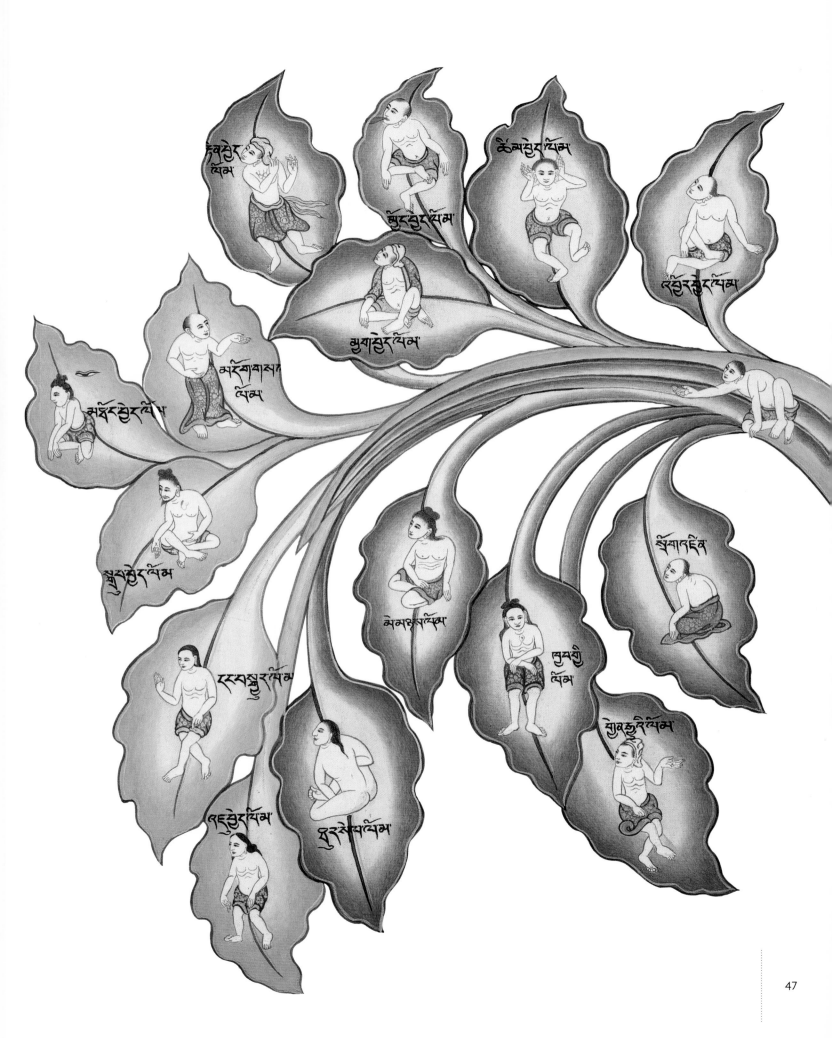

Human anatomy

Anatomical knowledge in Tibet was acquired from the examination of corpses at sky-burial sites on rocky prominences high above the plateau. Bodies were dissected, the bones crushed and, in religious rites conferring the body's constituent elements to the sky, offered to vultures and other birds of prey. Tibetans were well aware that the true body was not to be found amid the flesh and bones. As Karma Chagmey Rinpoche said, 'If you do not make use of this body, it will be lost in no time . . . So take advantage of it now and realize its essential nature.'

Cadaver

right

Crowned by the heart, this image displays organs, bones and viscera as they were observed at sky-burial sites.

Cranial physiognomy

opposite

Depicting the circulation of the blood throughout the body, this thangka also illustrates cranial types. Beginning in the upper right corner, a head with an elongated crown is shown, indicating a predominance of Wind; a head with a prominent occiput indicates Bile, while a square head signifies Wind and Bile in combination. A broad head indicates Phlegm and Wind, a round head Phlegm and Bile, a triangular head Phlegm, and a head with a flat crown a combination of all three humours.

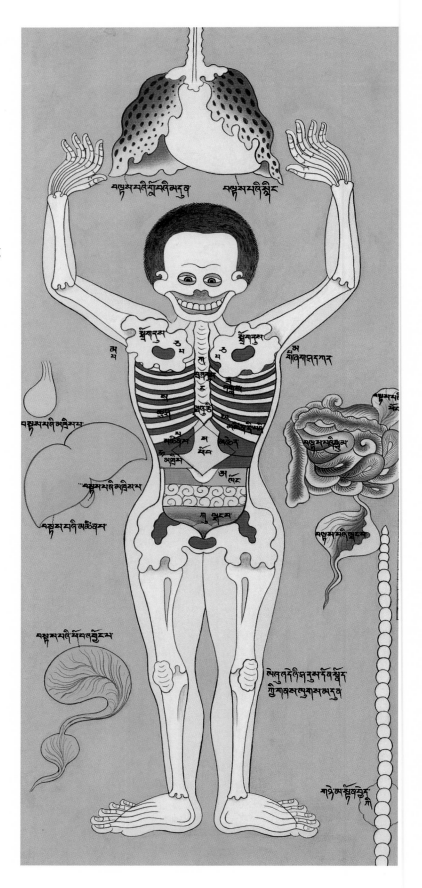

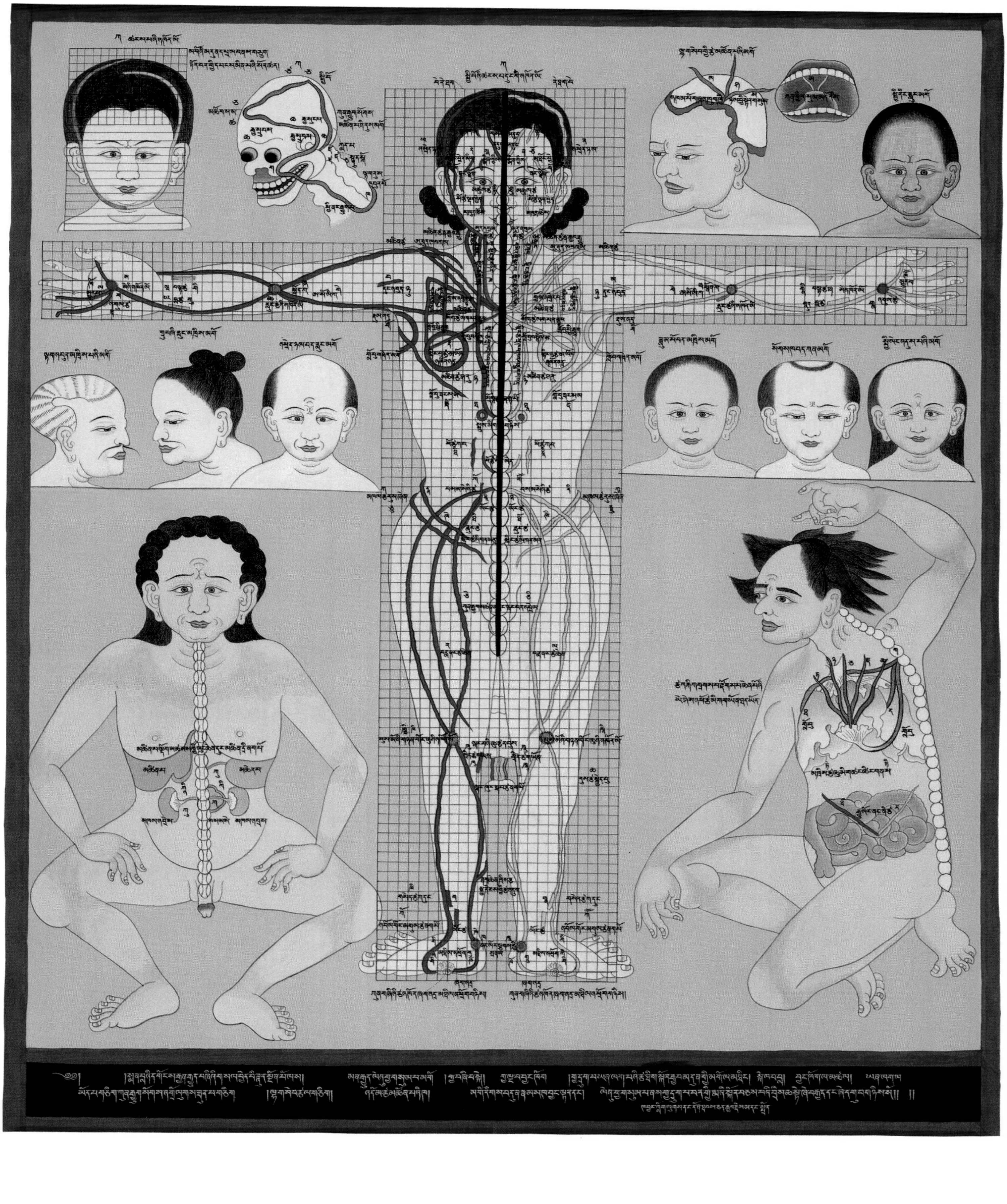

Metaphors of the body

Anatomical dissection alone can never yield the body's true proportions, still less its subtle bio-energetic structures and their interrelationship. Metaphors enlarge our sense of possibility and free us from constraining literalism. To imagine the body as a palace or its internal elements as a mandala is to see the world symbolically with openness and presence. In early Buddhism, to break excessive attachment, the body was meditated upon as a 'sack of filth' or, at best, as an impermanent dwelling. In the Tantras, however, the body is prized as the 'jewel ship' of awakening consciousness. These metaphors lead us to recognize that we create ourselves according to our own fears and ideals. As Tharthang Tulku suggests, 'The body's solidity is a mere appearance reflecting a limitation of our powers of observation.' To free it, he says, inspect

The body as a palace

below

The preciousness of the human body and the interrelationship of its internal components is illustrated in a medical thangka describing the physical body in similes of palace architecture. In the detail shown the upper panel compares the hip bones to foundation walls, the vertebrae to a stack of gold coins from the treasury, the channel of life to an agate pillar, the breast bone to a cross-beam, and the ribs to well-laid rafters. Tendons and ligaments are likened to ceiling planks and muscle and skin to plaster. The lower panel shows shoulder-blades as lateral buttresses and the head like a turret or roof-top shrine with the various sense organs arrayed as ornaments.

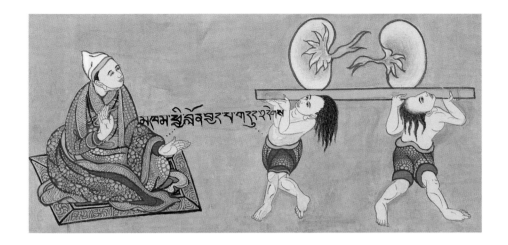

the body's structures, 'moving through its defining surfaces until they become completely open. . . . Allow them to remain as shining outlines . . . try to see the body from all directions and levels simultaneously.' Consciously or unconsciously, we are the creators of our own reality.

The subtle body

Our physical form arises from a subtle-energy body originating at the navel. The 'channels of formation' rise to generate the brain, descend to create the genitals, and flow through the neural tube to generate the 'channel of life'. The etheric energy system encased within our physical bodies, Tibetans claim, is the source not only of physical existence, but the 'wish-fulfilling jewel' which awakens our innermost 'Body of Truth'.

Chakras and energy channels

below and opposite

The Buddhist Tantras describe a network of 72,000 subtle-energy channels branching out in finer and finer configurations throughout the body's 'inner mandala'. The central channel, which begins at the sexual organs and ascends to the point between the eyebrows, is flanked by two side channels called *roma* and *kyangma* which circulate the body's 'solar' and 'lunar' energies. Linking them are the five primary *tsakhor*, or channel wheels, situated at the genitals, the navel, the heart, the throat and the crown of the head. It is at these vital centres that the causal body and physical body intersect and where through the practices of Tantric yoga the body's inner elements can be refined into their subtle essences. As Lama Sangwa stated, 'By causing the winds and subtle drops to enter into the central channel, bliss arises and the body itself becomes the source of enlightened awareness.'

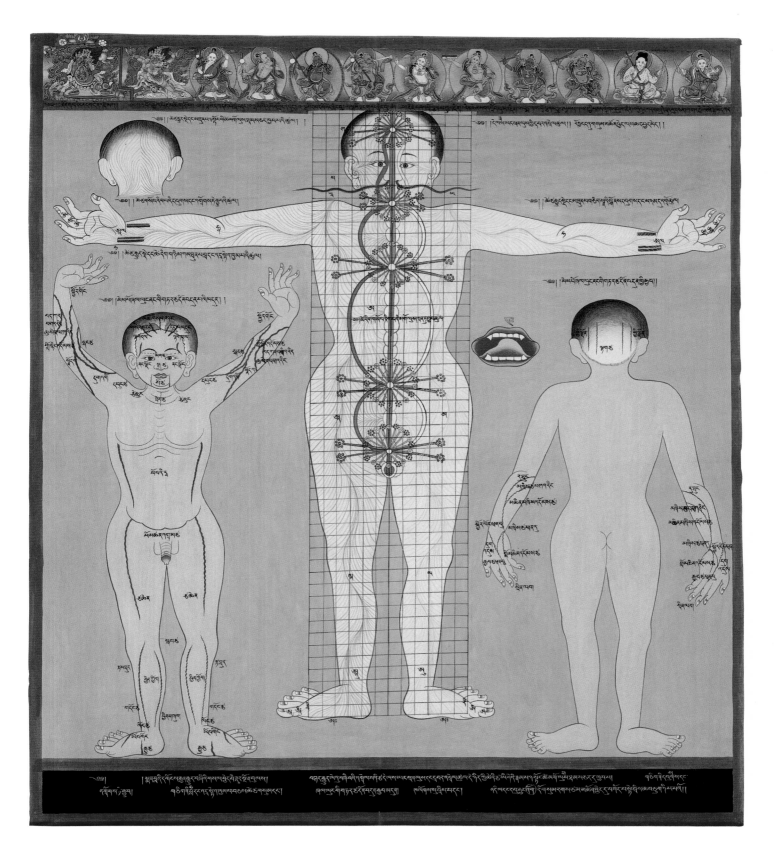

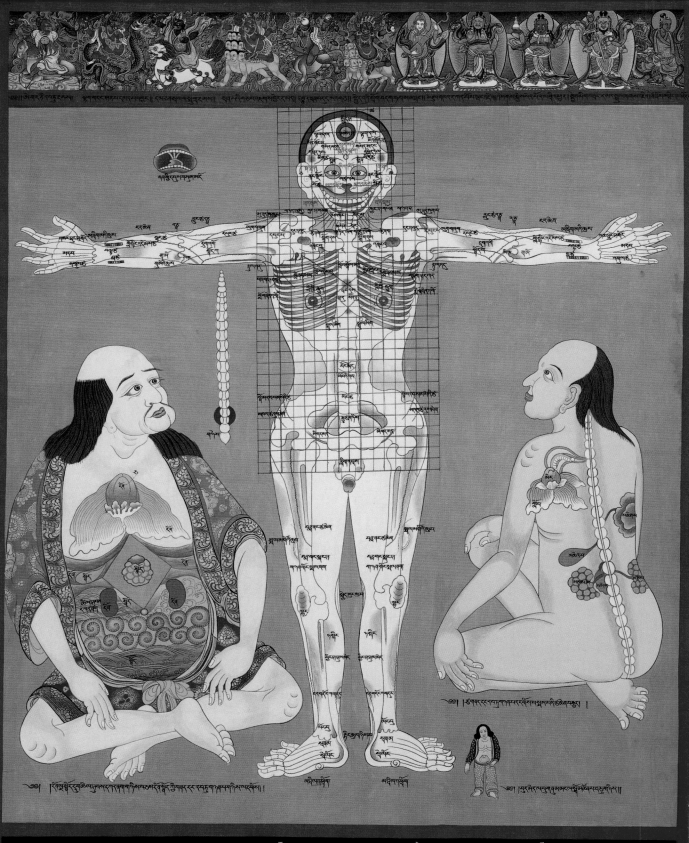

Throughout life we experience an inevitable and unalterable process of physiological change. The human body grows, ages and dies regardless of human will or intervention. Whether we die enmeshed within our hopes and fears or free ourselves by recognizing the selfless luminosity of our innermost being, impermanence lies at the heart of all existence. At the sky-burial site at Drigung Monastery, a maroon-robed yogi pounds the bones of a fresh corpse while vultures shift anxiously on the nearby rocks. 'Whether in illness or health, life or death,' the yogi states, 'the body is the greatest teacher of impermanence.' Offering to the birds that to which we have been most attached – our physical bodies – is a practce believed by Tibetans to hold great spiritual merit. Within minutes the last remnants of the corpse have been consumed, and the great birds fly off into the brightness of the horizon.

Vulnerable points

opposite

This thangka illustrates sensitive areas of the human body where injury can be life-threatening. From the 302 points that are specifically indicated, 95 are muscles, bones, tendons, veins and nerves located in the neck and head. The same number of vulnerable points can be found in the trunk, while the limbs have 112. Classified into three groups, according to their level of vulnerability, the body's most critical points include the thirteen solid and hollow viscera, the eight adipose glands, and the thirteen white channels (nerves) referred to as the 'hanging silk threads'.

Three stages of life

below

'In the end my body will turn to dust;
Unable to move by itself,
It will be propelled by other forces.
Why do I grasp this frail and
ephemeral form as "I".'

Shantideva

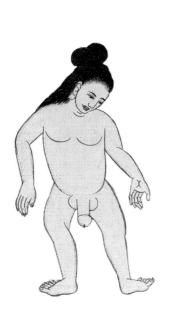

2 Disease: encountering pain

The Buddha's first teaching concerned the Truth of Universal Suffering. Before embarking on the path of healing and liberation, the Buddha taught, one must experience fully the discomfiting reality of pain and dissatisfaction. The afflictions of the body offer perhaps the most profound window on this perennial truth. Only by contemplating our own and others' mortality can we acquire true wisdom and compassion. For it is our rigid conception of who we are that suffers most when we fall ill. In Buddhist thought, disease presents us with a unique opportunity to experience more deeply our interconnectedness with other beings. The images of illness and disease portrayed in the medical paintings lead us into a visceral encounter with suffering and the healing response that arises from recognizing our mortality. As Buddha said, the contemplation of disease, especially our own, urges us into compassion and the sudden possibility of wholeness and integration.

Disease and its origins

opposite

A thangka entitled 'The Wondrous Synopsis' illustrates sections of the Blue Beryl pertaining to disease and pathology. The panels depict the diverse causes which lead to illness, including seasonal imbalances, defects in diet and behaviour, accidents and ripening karma. Deriving from the Indo-Nepalese artistic tradition, the series of horizontal panels which form the basis of many of the medical paintings are designed not only to impart technical information, but also to be pleasing to the eye.

Theft of the life-force

left

'Like an enemy waiting in ambush, disease comes without warning.'

Sangwa Tulku

The three primordial afflictions

In Tibetan medicine, disease in its most pervasive and chronic form is attributed to a basic ignorance of the interdependent origin of all phenomena and the true nature of the self. From this primal ignorance arise desire and aggression which betray, respectively, feelings of incompleteness and inner poverty and a deluded sense of threat and separation. Such mental confusion creates physiological stress and thus gives rise to states of inner imbalance. In the words of Dr Lobsang Rapgay, 'Though the mind cannot directly produce physical form, negative feelings such as envy, hatred and fear, when they become habitual, are capable of starting organic changes within our bodies.'

Although Tibetan medicine acknowledges the influence of pathogens, improper diet and behaviour in creating disease, the forces of grasping and aggression rooted in human ignorance are considered the three primordial afflictions from which all others stem. According to the medical Tantras, 'There is but one cause for all disease – the ignorance of not understanding the absence of an abiding self-identity. . . . Even when a bird soars in the sky, it is not parted from its shadow. Likewise, even when human beings live with joy, because of ignorance they are never free of illness.'

Ignorance, greed, aggression

above

Symbolized by a bird, a snake and a wild pig, the primordial human afflictions of greed, aggression and sloth are considered by Tibetan medicine to initiate physiological changes within our bodies and to be at the root of all physical, emotional and mental illness. In their subtlest form, the three 'mind poisons' manifest themselves as persistent indifference to the openness and fluidity that underlie all existence.

The leaves of discontent

opposite

'The hunger of the passions is the greatest disease. Disharmony is the greatest sorrow. When you know this well, then you know, too, that Nirvana is the only lasting joy'

Dhammapada

Rooted in Buddhist philosophy which reveals the subtle sense of discontent underlying our pursuit of happiness, Tibetan medicine explores the close interrelationship between physical and mental suffering and the sense of estrangement that characterizes bodily existence. As the Dalai Lama wrote, 'Since time immemorial our intrinsic Buddha-Nature has been obscured by the forces of ignorance, greed and aggression, as symbolized by the pig, the cockerel and the snake. . . . These negative mental impulses obscure our limitless potential and are the root cause of our frustrating transmigrations through cyclic existence.' Recognizing these three 'mind poisons' in their subtlest incarnations provides insight into the origins of all disease, for acknowledging their influence is the first step in developing wisdom. As Buddha himself is said to have stated, 'All life is suffering. When one sees this clearly, suffering ceases to exist.'

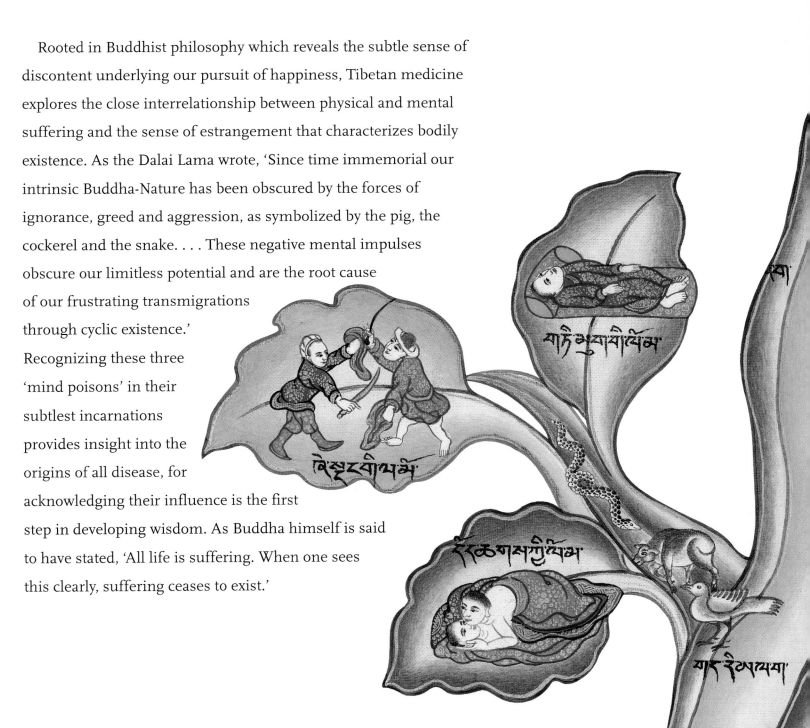

61

Imbalance of the elements

Buddhist medical theory holds that ignorance, greed and aggression resonate at the level of the body's cells, causing imbalances in the corresponding humours of Phlegm, Bile and Wind and the elements upon which they are based. Representing in their essential form the forces of consciousness, metabolism and inert matter within the human body, the three humours are, when balanced, sources of health and well-being. When their natural functions are disturbed, however, they equally cause disease.

Desire and grasping are said to produce imbalances in the body's air element, corresponding to the psycho-physical process of Wind. Anger and hostility create disturbances in the fire element corresponding to Bile, and indifference and sloth disturb the elements of earth and water which are related to Phlegm. Imbalances are caused not only by the subtle effects of the three 'mind poisons', but also through environmental influences, improper diet, trauma and infection. As all of these have as their basis the principles of earth, water, fire, air and space, disease will occur when, from whatever cause, the balance between these five primordial elements is disrupted.

When the body's air element is disturbed, mental disorders, nervousness and depression can arise, as well as heart conditions linked to stress. When the fire element is affected, the body becomes susceptible to skin and liver diseases, headaches and mental torpor. Disturbances of the earth and water elements can produce chronic digestive problems, as well as influenza and swelling of the joints. Disturbance of the body's inner elements represents a mingling of physical and psychological factors – a model of the profound interdependence of mind and body.

The routes of imbalance

right

When the inner elements become unbalanced, diseases of the three humours move through the body following specific pathways. The uppermost five leaves illustrate the areas affected by pathogenic Wind. The outermost leaves show the pathways of disordered Bile, while the five leaves on the lower section of the upper branch reveal the routes associated with unbalanced Phlegm. The seasons, environments, and stages of life when imbalances of specific humours are likely to occur are symbolized in the branch below.

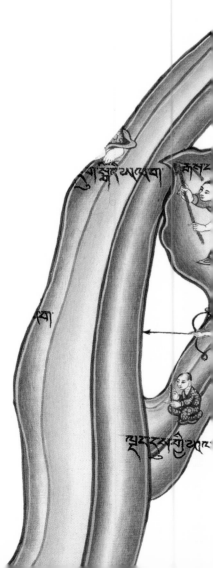

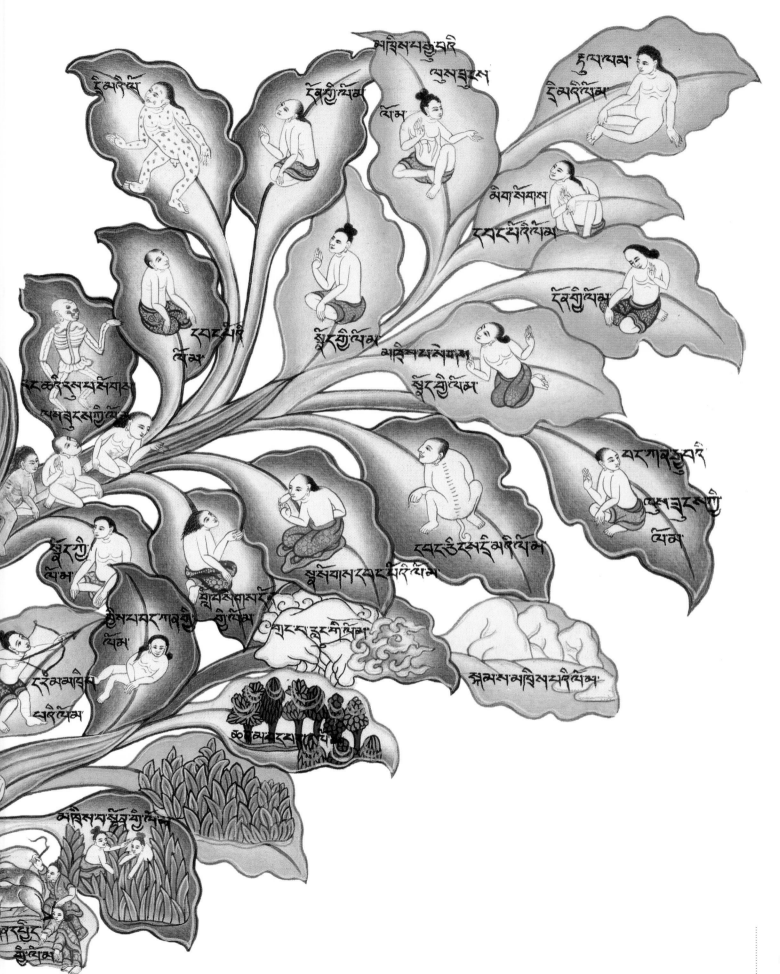

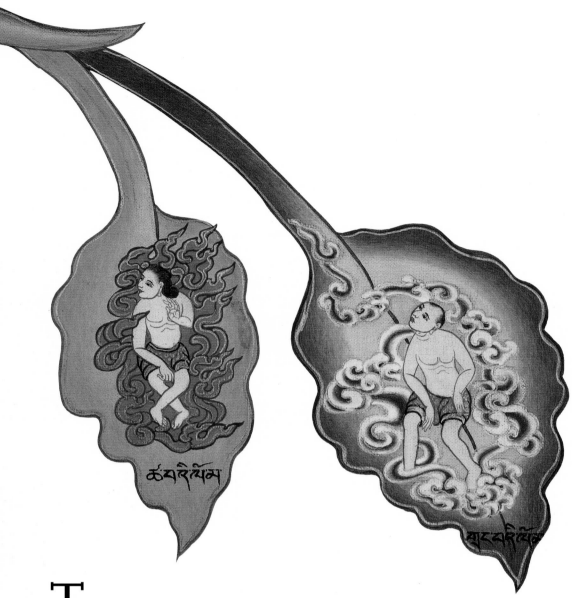

The figures illustrated in Tibetan medical paintings show three standing male figures, each associated with Tibetan script captions: ཚ་བའི་ལུས (left) and གྲང་བའི་ལུས (right).

The medical Tantras list four categories of disease. The first includes karmic illnesses resulting from negative actions in past lives; the second diseases caused by spirits; the third self-limiting illnesses that disappear spontaneously; and the fourth imbalances of the humours caused by harmful food and behaviour, by pathogens and by environmental stress. As Namkha Amchi stated, 'If we learn to recognize the underlying causes of disease, we begin to learn how to restore balance. Until then disease is our constant companion . . . If you wish to find happiness, look into the nature of suffering. Unless we do, it is like trying to run away from our own shadow.'

Diseases of heat and cold

left

In Tibetan diagnostic theory, all diseases can be broadly categorized as either 'hot' or 'cold' or a complicated combination of both. Hot disorders are caused by an increase in the Bile humour. Cold diseases generally result from an imbalance of Phlegm or Wind.

Diseases of excess

opposite above

Diseases of the humours are classified according to whether the imbalance causes a condition of excess, of deficiency, or a mutual aggravation. As indicated here, an excess of Wind can result in darkening of the skin, emaciation, trembling, weakness, vertigo and frequent chatter. An excess of Bile causes yellowing of the urine, skin and eyes, as well as fever, hunger and thirst. An excess of Phlegm manifests itself in chills, indigestion, breathlessness, lethargy, looseness of the joints, torpor and depression.

Patterns of distress

opposite below

The figures illustrated show the parts of the body where diseases of the humours typically begin: Wind disorders in the skeletal system; diseases of Bile in the blood and perspiration; and those of Phlegm in the skin and muscle tissue, from where they enter the ligaments, bones and internal organs.

Forest of symptoms

Certain paintings from the Blue Beryl illustrate disease and pathology using the metaphor of trees with branches and leaves symbolizing categories and symptoms of physiological imbalance. The medical Tantras define an unhealthy body as one in which the inner potential for illness meets the appropriate conditions for disease to manifest itself. Of the 404 diseases and 84,000 afflictions specified in the Tibetan medical Tantras, some affect only women and others only men. Some diseases are specific to childhood and others to old age. A 'cold' disorder in the lower part of the body may arise concurrently with a 'hot' disorder in the upper regions.

However it is described or is brought about, disease has the effect of disrupting our normal routines and acts as an incentive for us to reassess our lives. Sogyal Rinpoche wrote that 'The times when you are suffering can be those when you are most open, and where you are extremely vulnerable can be where your greatest strength really lies. . . . Suffering can, after all, teach us about compassion. If you suffer, you will know what it is like when others suffer. And if you are in a position to help others, it is through your own suffering that you will find the understanding and compassion to do so.'

opposite

Branches and leaves form an arboreal flow-chart depicting symptoms characteristic of disorders in the body's three psycho-physiological processes, or humours. The upper branch illustrates symptoms associated with disordered Wind, including yawning, stretching, shivering, aching limbs, nausea, dullness of the senses and mental agitation. The branch below shows symptoms connected to Bile disorders, including bitter eructations, headaches, fevers, and acute pains in the upper body. The first leaf on the lower branch illustrates the secondary causes of diseases of Phlegm, which include a diet that is heavy and oily. The subsequent leaves show loss of appetite, digestive problems and vomiting associated with disorders of this humour.

Transforming pain

Attachment, aversion and indifference are the underlying mental dispositions that cause imbalance in our internal energies and predispose us to disease. Tibetan doctors say that disease gives greater insight into the inner workings of the mind than does good health. When disease arises, if we look into its nature with equanimity we can recognize the mental attitudes that give rise to stress and physiological imbalance. Disease and suffering, even our own darkest habits, are highly instructive if we look inward with wisdom and compassion. In the same way that particular mental habits lead to disease, they can also be used to overcome it.

One of the most profound Tibetan Buddhist meditations is that of *tonglen*, 'giving and receiving'. In this practice one inhales the suffering of all humanity and exhales one's own well-being. This is done not only when one feels strong and in good health, but also in the midst of illness. As lamas explain, you should not try to imagine that your own pain is vanishing, but rather that you take on even more pain, representing the sufferings of all sentient

beings. When you do this, the body relaxes into its natural state and your own pain strangely begins to diminish. Sogyal Rinpoche has recommended that 'Whatever you do, do not shut off your pain; accept your pain and remain vulnerable. However desperate you become, accept your pain as it is, because it is in fact trying to hand you a priceless gift – the chance of discovering, through spiritual practice, what lies behind sorrow.'

Vitiating habits

above

Among the various conditions considered harmful to health, the Blue Beryl includes consumption of excessive amounts of salt, meat and alcohol and a sedentary lifestyle. In Sangwa Tulku's words, 'If you really want to overcome the root causes of suffering, look at your most cherished habits. Then give them up.'

'Day and night one feeds one's body
Yet only misery and confusion ensue. . . .
A melancholy scene, living beings
overpowered by craving and delusion.'

Seventh Dalai Lama

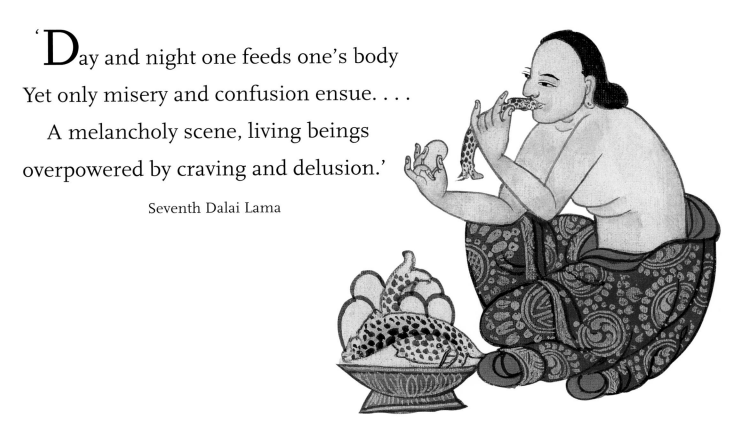

'Look closely and contemplate deeply
The people and things that appear around you. . . .
All are in constant flux.
Everything becomes the teacher of impermanence.'

Seventh Dalai Lama

'When you are strong and healthy,
You never think of sickness coming,
But it descends with sudden force
Like a stroke of lightning.'

Milarepa

ཕྲག་ཏུ་ཡེལ།   ཤ་ཏུ་ཡེལ།   ཚིལ་ཏུ་ཡེལ།

མེ་དཔལ་ལ་འདར་བ།

སུད་ཡ་ལ་ཟིན་པ།

ཟེག་ནད།

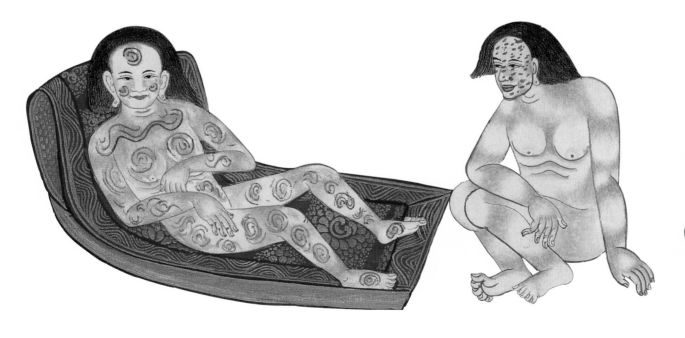

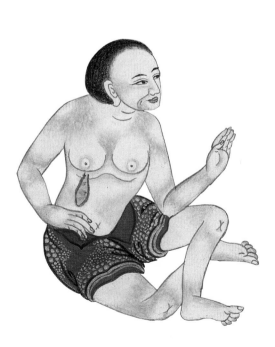

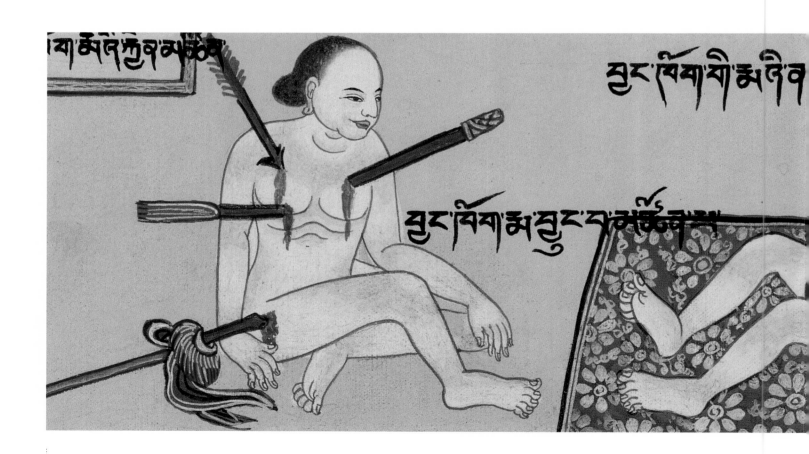

As early as the eighth century, Tibetan physicians anticipated the future proliferation of diseases caused by chemical toxins and environmental pollutants. According to Dr Tenzin Choedhak, personal physician to His Holiness the Dalai Lama, the appearance of eighteen new diseases (including meningitis, cancer and conditions affecting the body's immune system) was predicted, all of them being based on the increasing disharmony between the elements of the human body and the external environment.

Naturally occurring poisons such as snake venom, as well as the viruses carried by malarial mosquitoes, are described in the medical Tantras, along with the harmful effects of prolonged exposure to the sun. Nine specific poisonous plants are listed, including datura (thorn apple) and poison ivy. The medical texts also refer to the toxins inherent in decomposing meat, as well as those created by improper combinations of otherwise nutritious foods – fish and eggs, milk and radishes being primary examples. Present-day Tibetan physicians also refer to the toxic effects of chemical additives in processed foods.

Although poisons are referred to as a source of disease, they are also regarded in Tantric medicine, when used in their purified state and in the right dosage, as the basis of potent remedies. For example, aconite and mercury in homoeopathic dilution can cure disease by stimulating the body's own vital force. The same is said of the three 'mind poisons' – ignorance, desire and aggression. When purified by seeing directly into their essential nature, these same disabling passions become potent sources of insight and healing energy.

The origin of poisons

opposite

This thangka illustrates the mythological origins of poisons, ascribing them to a fanged, snake-garlanded entity that emerged from the depths of the primeval sea. Shattered by mantras intoned by a retinue of gods, Kalakuta's toxins were dispersed throughout the natural world. The first of the four lower panels depicts the sources of naturally occurring and compounded poisons, including tainted meat, weasels, frogs, scorpions, mountain lizards, snakes and ultra-violet radiation. The other three illustrate the diverse ways in which poisons can be transmitted, ending with a man who has fallen victim to the bite of a rabid dog.

Sorcery and malevolent spirits

According to Tibetan medical theory, those whose minds have not yet attained to clarity and wisdom are subject to environmental influences perceived as demonic. Whether conjured up by ill-willed sorcerers or happened upon accidentally, diseases brought about by malevolent spirits are by no means uncommon. Dr Yeshi Donden stated that 'I could not even count the number of people who have been affected by spirits. . . . Even though they cannot be seen, spirits definitely do exist and bring harm.'

Contagion of place

left

Certain environments, such as the workplaces of butchers and blacksmiths, are considered inherently defiling. The negative spiritual energies encountered in such places can result in diseases that are difficult to diagnose, presenting symptoms that resemble those resulting from allergies.

Plague-causing spirits

below

According to the Blue Beryl, prolonged and misdirected rituals can disturb disease-causing entities within the environment. Pictured here are water spirits called nagas, a local earth spirit referred to as a *sadag*, and a mundane deity whose armour serves to symbolize his belligerent nature.

Acts of sorcery

above and left

Spirits are believed to exist as emanations of the physical environment. Invoked through rituals, their essentially neutral energies can be enlisted to prevent disease or, as pictured here, directed against an enemy bringing illness and misfortune.

The influence of demons

T ibet's pre-Buddhist shamanistic tradition animates mind and nature with unseen forces and energies. Although Buddhism dismisses demons as mental projections, malevolent spirits remain symbolic of a vast range of emotions. Demons fall into two categories – those born of hope and those born of fear; each is expressive of our resistance to the impermanence of all experience. As Trungpa Rinpoche explained, 'Those things which we want excluded from our lives are the demons; those things which we would draw towards us are the gods and goddesses.'

Demons of childhood

below

According to Tibetan medical science, there are fifteen demons which cause nervous disorders in children. Pictured here are the dog-faced demon who causes trembling, the preta-faced demon with open mouth who causes shortness of breath, the bird-faced demoness who engenders fever, the demoness of decomposition who causes diarrhoea and hiccups, the cold and blind demonesses of decomposition responsible for shivering and defects of vision, the broad-faced demoness who causes loss of appetite, and the blue rabbit-eared demoness Revati who turns a child's complexion blue.

Child plagued by demons

above

Emanating from a visionary realm, demons can be the source of myriad ailments regarded by modern medical opinion as imaginary and incurable.

Demons

right

Whether symbols of psychic energies or actual entities dwelling beyond our current awareness, demons open the mind to subconscious forces.

Madness and mental disorders

In Tibetan medical theory, pathological disturbances of mind and spirit arise through imbalances in the body's inner elements resulting from exposure to poisons, excessive grief and anxiety, mental strain, as well as ripening karma and demonic possession. Depending on the causes of mental illness in individual patients, the treatment recommended ranges from changes in diet and behaviour to acupuncture, moxibustion, herbal remedies, exorcism and shamanistic rites. In extreme cases of madness, the only

Causes of insanity

below

The first panel shows derangements in the psycho-physical elements symbolized by a demon intruding into the central channel and disturbing the energy pathways that are associated with consciousness and rational thought. Preconditions for madness are seen in the lower panel; here, demonic possession is depicted in the person of a deranged sword-wielding monk.

effective remedy is the application of the dried blood of a murder victim, a substance more potent than fantasies and deluded fears, to the patient's lips.

For Tantric practitioners who abandon conventional definitions of reality, madness is a perennial risk, hence awareness of the empty nature of all phenomena becomes an absolute prerequisite. In this visionary realm, the fine line between mental disorders and self-realization was pointed out by Sangwa Tulku: 'If one's thoughts concern oneself, it is mental disease. If they concern the welfare of others, it is crazy wisdom, no matter how eccentric one's behaviour may appear on the surface.'

Imaginary diseases

above and below

One hundred and one physical and psychiatric diseases are attributed to the effects of demonic interference. In addition to the use of medications which correct imbalances in the body's neurochemistry, treatment consists of magical rites determined on the basis of urine analysis and examination of the patient's pulses.

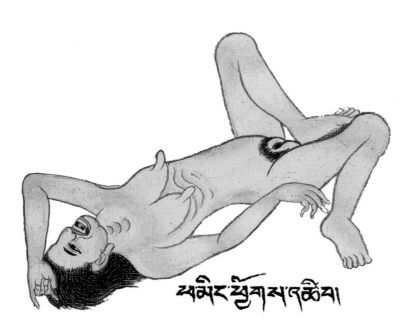

Diseases of the life span

above

A dragon swallowing the sun and moon symbolizes life-threatening diseases which, if left untreated, will result in death. Circumstances in which disease may be fatal include cases where a prescribed medicine is not taken or an ignorant physician administers a single medication for a hundred different diseases. The second panel shows cases of complex fever which must be treated as if constructing a dam as protection against the threat of flooding. In other circumstances treatment should resemble the protection offered to a caravan by armed merchants. For diseases arising from past karma, no medicine is effective and the patient will inevitably die.

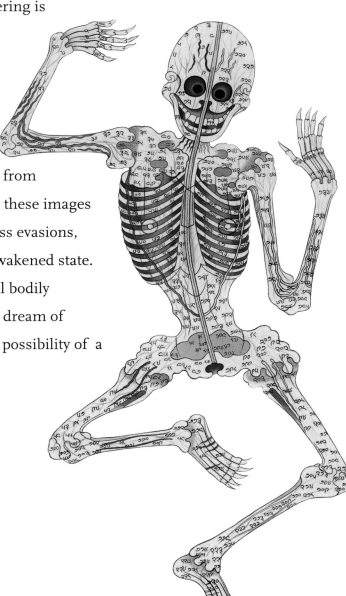

Death and terminal illness confront us with the impermanence of our physical bodies and the fleeting nature of all existence. If denied or repressed, such awareness can lead to madness and depression. Integrated, it leads to liberation from the fears and untenable hopes that contract our lives. The contemplation of suffering is the foundation of the Buddhist path. Encountering the symptoms and sources of disease, from cancer to primordial unrest, attachments diminish and compassion grows. The demons, skeletons and spectral apparitions – the iconography of fear which dominates Tantric art – are designed to free us from unintegrated, fragmented perception. Until we admit these images into our consciousness, our lives will consist of endless evasions, never attaining to the clarity and spontaneity of the awakened state. Serving as an icon of the essential truth underlying all bodily existence, a smiling skeleton reveals our unrealizable dream of permanence and leads us into what lies beyond – the possibility of a radical wholeness to which suffering cannot attain.

The face of impermanence

left

'Life and death are in the mind and nowhere else. Mind is . . . the universal basis of all experience – the creator of happiness and the creator of suffering, the creator of what we call life and what we call death.'

Sogyal Rinpoche

Dancing in the void

right

'When finally your life forces disintegrate,
Watch the elements of the body dissolve.
Then, like remeeting an old friend,
Eagerly greet the clear light of death.'

Seventh Dalai Lama

3 Diagnosis: developing wisdom

As ignorance is regarded as the primary cause of all suffering, healing begins with insight into the sources of our distress. The second Noble Truth taught by the Buddha was the origin of suffering, which he revealed as rooted in a fragmentary understanding of our human condition. Similarly, in medicine, before an illness can be alleviated or cured, its nature must be fully comprehended. Achieving this goal is the function of diagnosis, literally to see through or into, or – as it is known in Tibetan medicine – *ngozen*, to 'recognize or identify'.

Diagnosis in Tibetan medicine is oriented more towards ways of knowing and understanding the processes of disease than to the analysis of the microscopic qualities of specific pathogenic organisms. As Dr Lobsang Dolma stated, 'There are no optical, acoustic or computer-based instruments of diagnosis – only the trained senses of the physician. These are developed over a period of many years and directed towards the examination of a patient's pulse and urine.'

By sensitizing oneself to become aware of subtle imbalances in the body's energy patterns and attending to seasonal influences, circumstances and behaviour that could otherwise result in disease can be largely avoided. As Tibetans say, awareness of the causes of disease leads not just to prevention and cure; it also represents the first step in developing wisdom.

When disease does arise, Tibetan doctors urge the patient to look deeply into its causes so as to transform it into a source of insight. As Tsampa Amchi said, 'Only by experiencing the roots of suffering can one clearly determine the nature of disease and develop the qualities of a healer.'

The three stems of inquiry

opposite

In a tree illustrating the diverse approaches to diagnosis employed in the Tibetan medical system, the branches on the lower left show how the tongue reveals states of imbalance in the three bodily humours, while the branch above indicates the methods used in analyzing urine. The central stem illustrates palpation of the pulse, the primary diagnostic technique in Tibetan medicine. The third stem is subdivided into three additional branches, each illustrating the symptoms and curative regimens for diseases of the three humours.

Tongue diagnosis

below

Examination of a patient's tongue originates from the Chinese medical tradition: a parched and shrivelled tongue indicates a Wind disorder accompanied by severe fever.

Before prescribing an appropriate therapeutic regimen, a Tibetan doctor must thoroughly understand the underlying causes of a patient's illness. Dr Yeshe Donden has observed that 'The Western scientist looks through a microscope to examine the cause of disease in terms of its molecular particles. Only then does he take into account the particular characteristics of the patient. Tibetan doctors begin with the patient.'

Roots of healing

below left

Diagnosis of disease in the Tibetan medical system consists primarily of visual observation, urine analysis, examination of the pulse and verbal questioning, as illustrated by this grouping of physicians and patients at the base of a tree.

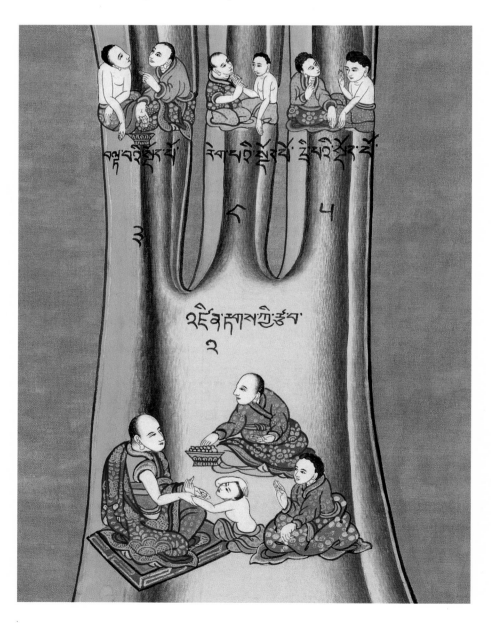

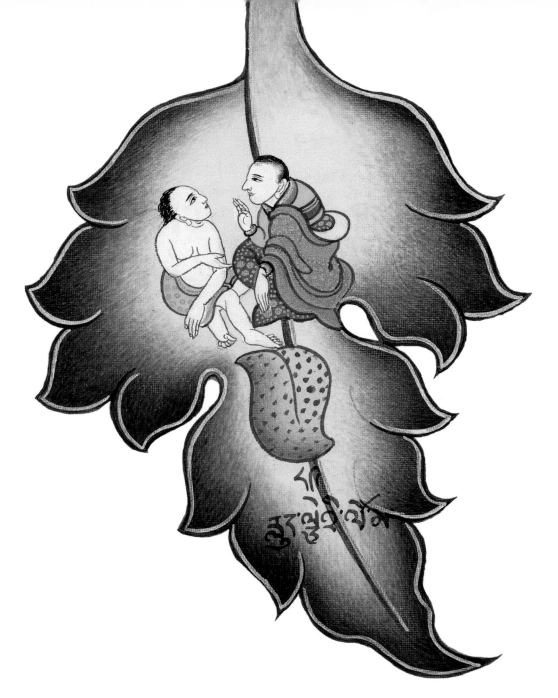

The tongue under Wind imbalance

left

Details from the Tibetan medical paintings function more as mnemonic images and sources of inspiration than they do as exacting illustrations of pathological states. In all aspects, information revealed through these images was supplemented by the oral teachings of master physicians. For purposes of diagnosis, the tip of the tongue corresponds to disorders in the chest cavity, while the middle section and root refer, respectively, to the upper and lower abdomen. The physician examines colour, shape, texture and coating to determine the nature of disease.

Diagnostic procedures

below

In a panel illustrating the three primary approaches to diagnosis, a doctor is shown inspecting a patient's tongue, his physique, as well as a bowl of his urine. The second vignette shows palpation of the pulses, while the third illustrates his verbal inquiry into the causes, locations and symptoms of a patient's illness.

I n order to be able to assess correctly the causes of a particular disease, a competent doctor must be well-versed not only in the three primary diagnostic techniques, but he should also be skilled in carrying out secondary procedures which reveal the nature of specific disorders. In this way the physician avoids problems associated with over-medication or with the use of other counter-productive forms of

Diagnostic tests

left and centre

When a physician is uncertain about the exact nature of a disease, he may test for any suspected disorders by administering a variety of decoctions. If the initial diagnosis was correct, the respective imbalances will subside without additional treatment.

Diagnostic procedures

below

The preliminary test for digestive disorders, indicating the measure of purgatives required, is a decoction of chebula. The test indicating the need for moxibustion is the application of a warm oily compress. To determine the efficacy of bloodletting, a cold stone is placed against the skin. To test whether or not pus is ready to be extracted from a swelling, a hot stylet should be placed against the affected area.

therapy. Depending on the physician's specific diagnosis, at the stage when diseases of the humours are gathering at their respective bodily locations,

tranquillizing medications should be administered. Cathartic procedures should be used only once the disease has surfaced. If the initial diagnosis was incorrect, rather than being helpful, the medicines prescribed may have a harmful effect or possibly lead to the development of other diseases. As Tsampa Amchi stated, 'Without a proper knowledge of the methods of diagnosis, treatment may only result in further complications. Such doctors are likened to wily foxes usurping the throne of kings.' The medical paintings include a variety of graphic metaphorical indications concerning the correct procedures to be followed.

Guidelines for physicians

above

'Proceeding without understanding the principles of diagnosis is likened to an archer shooting in the dark. Until the details of a particular case are established, proceed cautiously like a creeping cat. Once the diagnosis is firm, proceed decisively, as in hoisting a banner on a roof-top. If secondary ailments require treatment first, proceed as if goading an untrained horse. In treating a patient who has previously taken incorrect remedies and medications, proceed unerringly like a gull catching a fish.'

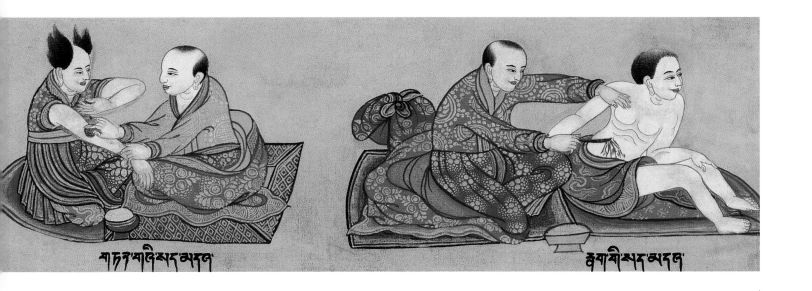

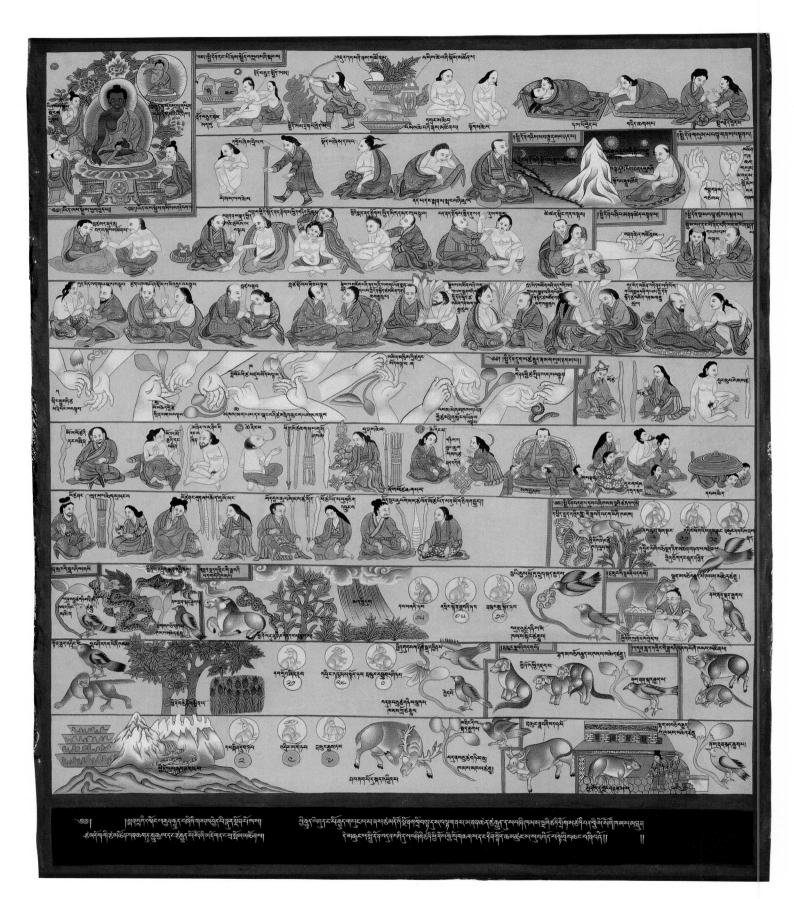

The art of pulse diagnosis is one of the most impressive and mystifying features of Tibetan medicine. Placing his fingers at specific points on a patient's wrists, the experienced physician attunes his consciousness to the subtle pulsations of blood, lymph and neural energies which convey messages regarding the patient's state of health and vitality. The upper and lower portions of the tips of the physician's three middle fingers exert varying degrees of pressure. Twelve individual readings reveal detailed information regarding imbalances in the patient's constitution. Described metaphorically as resembling 'the sound of water dripping in spring', 'the pecking of a hen eating grain', or 'the staggering of a crippled bird', the pulses reveal not only the state of an individual's physical, emotional and spiritual well-being, but, under the hands of the most adept physicians, are also said to serve as indicators of the life span of an individual and to reveal past and future events.

Techniques of diagnosis

opposite

The medical thangka introducing pulse diagnosis covers topics such as the time and place of examination, the pressure and positioning of the fingers, as well as seasonal influences and the characteristics of different constitutional pulses.

'Astonishing' pulses

below

Pulses can reveal not only one's own state of health, but also that of a relative. As shown here, a trained physician can diagnose the father's disease by examining the pulses of his son.

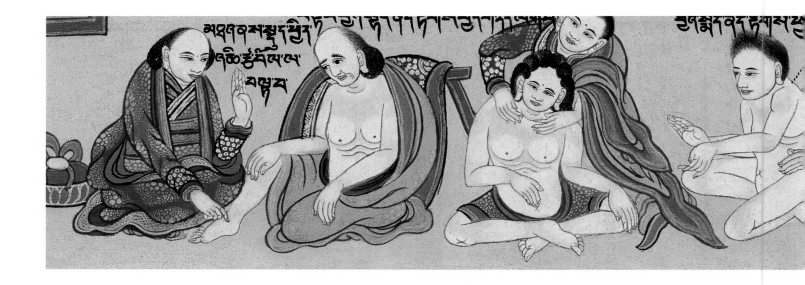

Tibetan physicians compare the pulsating waves of energy emanating at different points in the body to messengers conveying vital information about a patient's state of health. To examine the pulses associated with the internal organs, the physician places three fingers on the radial artery, thus tapping into the flow of vital energy radiating through the patient's body. As illustrated above, the pulse of impending death can be read on the dorsal arteries of the feet. The carotid arteries which carry blood to the head reveal external diseases of the upper body, while the femoral

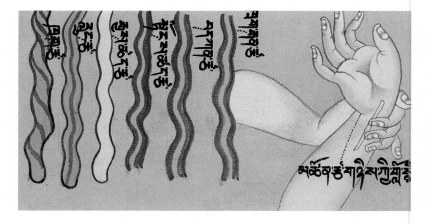

arteries in the groin and axillary arteries located in the armpit indicate diseases in the lower body. The pulsation of winds and blood at the heart centre determine the patient's probable life span.

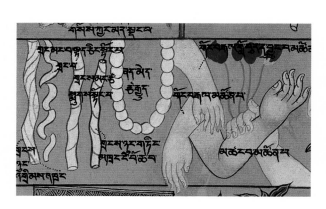

Pulse Rates

above

The physician measures the pulse rate in relation to his own breathing: In a healthy state the pulse beats twice during each exhalation, once during the respiratory pause, and twice again during inhalation. Each wrist is checked separately for a minimum of one hundred beats.

below left

Idiosyncrasies in the location and frequency of a healthy person's pulses can be easily mistaken for evidence of disease.

right
'A twisted pulse under the physician's middle finger indicates injury to the cranial bones. . . . An abnormally rapid pulse under the ring finger indicates injury to the brain.'

below
'A hermaphrodite or *bodhicitta* pulse . . . may be confused with a weak and slow pulse indicative of cold disease . . . An absent pulse or a pulse with interruptions and halts . . . with a pulse of impending death.'

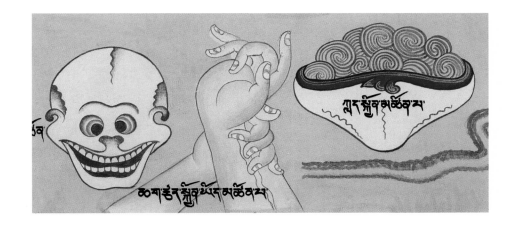

Divination through the pulses

Prophetic pulses

right

The Tibetan medical Tantras include chapters on complex forms of pulse diagnosis that foretell future events. On the right the depiction of a 'faint yet torrential pulse seemingly immobilized by its own strength' portends terrifying experiences for the person being examined.

Friend-Enemy pulses

above

In the 'Friend-Enemy' cycle of pulse divination, if friend pulses beat in the manner of their enemies, i.e. that of the spleen and earth element, this is an indication that personal wealth will be carried off by an adversary.

Astonishing pulses

right

A series of 'astonishing' pulses indicate the future course of an illness. Pictured here, an altered spleen pulse portends the harmful influence of a minor demon and auspicious circumstances for the patient's wife.

To the skilled practitioner of Tibetan medicine the pulses express subtle energies that are unmeasurable by Western science. Healers with exceptional sensitivity are said to be able to read in the pulses not only imbalances in bodily constitution, but intimations of impending events. Entering with heightened awareness into the patient's lymph, blood and nervous systems, the physician makes contact with his psyche, of which the body is the ephemeral expression. Although rarely practised today by conventional Tibetan physicians, pulse diagnosis is used by highly realized

Possession by spirits

left

In a subchapter of sphygmology, the medical Tantras describe the sudden and erratic irregularities in the pulse associated with bewitchment and demonic possession. Here, a short, weak and indistinct pulsation at the left wrist indicates possession by a female demon, the embodied form of predatory emotions.

Ill-omened pulses

overleaf

Abnormalities in the pulses reveal an illness's future development as well as impending death.

Spirits of attachment
below

Symbolizing a wide range of renegade psychic energies, demons can be diagnosed according to abnormalities in the flow, tension and strength of the pulse and its relationship to the prevailing element during a particular season. If in the spring season the kidney pulse shows irregularities indicating demonic possession, it suggests the harmful influence of ancestor spirits clinging to the house and properties of an earlier life.

lamas and Tibetan spirit mediums as an auxiliary means of reaching the patient's unconscious mind and transmitting healing energy. Lhamo, a Tibetan spirit medium, said that, 'When I place my fingers on a patient's wrists, images appear which arise not from my imagination but from the patient's own suppressed awareness.' Restoring these forces to consciousness, she suggests, not only reveals the underlying cause of disease but initiates the process of healing. In Sangwa Tulku's words, 'Genuine recognition of one's own imbalanced state is half of the cure!'

The pulses of birth and death

In Tibetan pulse diagnosis the life-force of two human beings is connected through the sense of touch. A doctor can examine a pregnant woman's pulse months before childbirth to determine the sex of the developing foetus. If desired, he can also prescribe medicines that are said to change a female foetus into a male one. The pulses of impending death are described vividly in the medical Tantras. Some are likened to a 'flag fluttering in the wind' and others to a 'vulture attacking a bird, which stops, plunges, beats its wings quickly, stops again and then resumes flight'. Another death pulse is described as resembling 'the saliva of a drooling cow, moving in the wind'. Throughout life the pulse is the hidden

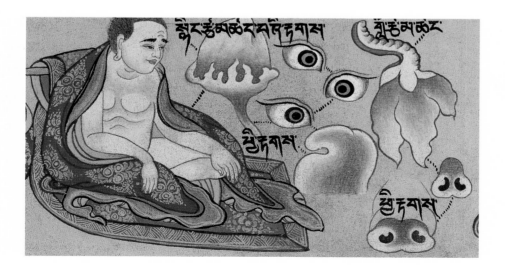

Pregnancy and childbirth

above

The pulse of a pregnant woman is described as protruding and rotatory. If, in addition, the right kidney pulse is stronger than the left, a boy will be born; if the left pulse is dominant, the child will be a girl. Complex pulse diagnoses can also be used to predict the outcome of childbirth, as well as the baby's future prospects.

Death pulses

below left

The absence of a heart pulse, as shown here, portends death if the external signs observed on the tongue and in the eyes provide corroboration. The absence of a lung pulse indicates imminent death if the nose appears pinched and its hairs point upwards.

opposite

Pulses portend death when their features do not conform with the nature of a particular disease or the patient's condition. The first figure illustrates a weak and thin pulse in a strong person affected by a sudden illness. A bulky and agitated pulse in a person who has suffered from a long debilitating illness also indicates impending death, as does a pulse suggesting fever in a cold disease and a pulse indicative of a cold disease which manifests itself during a fever.

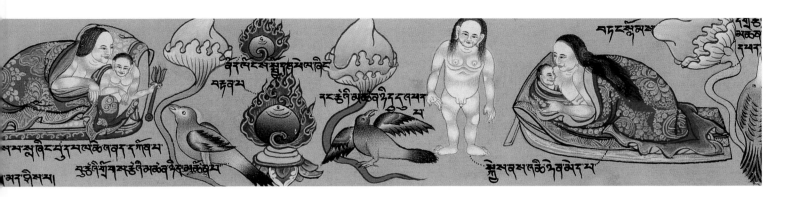

current whose movements
pattern our future lives.
As Dechen Amchi described it,
'the pulse is the bridge between
past and future . . . its rhythms
are those of impermanence,
openness, growth and
creativity.' As understood in
Tibetan Buddhism, the mysteries of birth and death initiate us
deeply into the pulse of life itself, into compassion – the capacity
to feel in unison with all sentient life.

Birth and death

left

If the son pulse should beat with the
characteristics of its enemy pulse,
childbirth will be complicated, the
mother will die, and the child will be
difficult to raise.

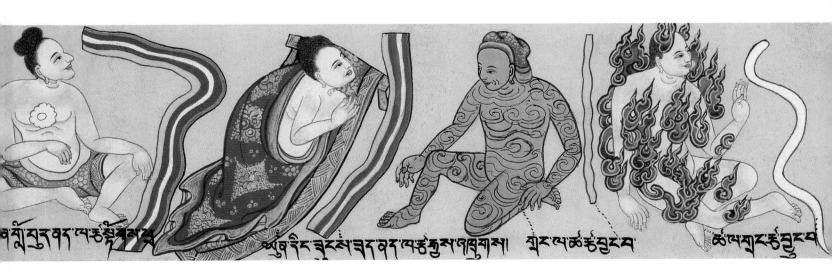

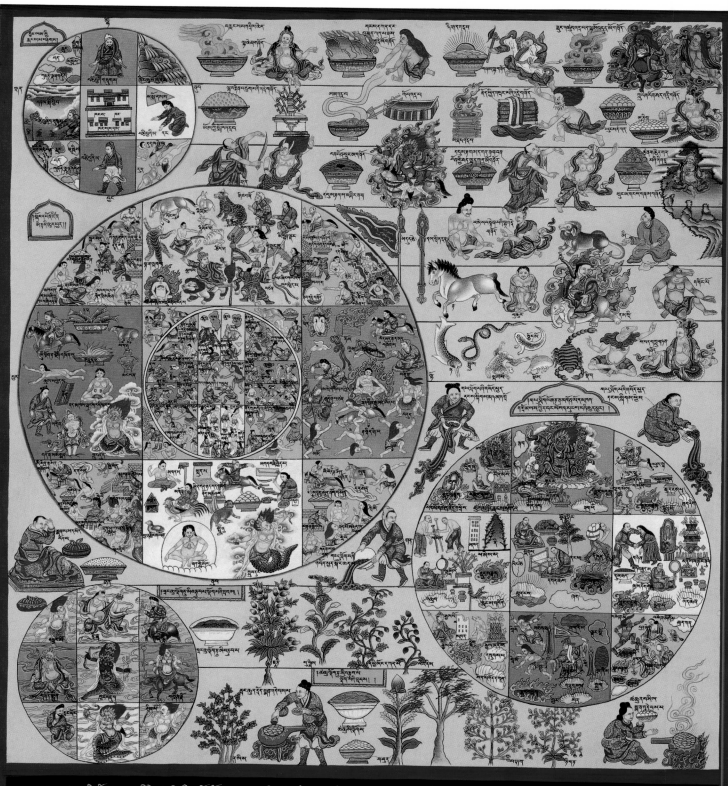

Water of life

opposite

The last in a series of paintings illustrating more conventional aspects of urine analysis, this highly intricate thangka reveals the methods and techniques used in examining urine for signs of demonic possession. The circular diagram in the top left-hand corner divides the specimen into nine sectors; the central one represents the household, while those surrounding it include agricultural fields, cemetery grounds and mountains. Eventual prognostications are based on the appearance of the urine vapours in the different sectors. In the complex diagram below, the inner circle represents the urine specimen in its container, while the outer sections show a plethora of geomantic and astrological elements which influence its appearance (see also p. 186). The divination chart illustrated in the lower right corner is associated with deities, ancestors and local spirits.

Time of inspection

above right

The urine sample should be collected at dawn when lunar and solar energies are in equilibrium. As illustrated, urine collected before 4 am is less suitable and should be discarded. In addition to the use of urine in diagnosing disease, appropriate dilutions of urine are prescribed to rectify conditions of deficient immunity.

Leaves of diagnosis

right

A detail from the Tree of Diagnosis illustrates the examination of urine from a patient affected by imbalances of the three humours.

In Tibetan medicine all but 5% of known diseases are said to be clearly identifiable from pulse diagnosis alone. In those cases where doubt exists, examination of the urine will reveal which of various possible diseases is actually present. Commenting on the combined efficacy of these two primary methods of diagnosis, Dr Lobsang Dolma stated that 'In Tibet we have a saying: "Touching and seeing, everything is known".'

Relying only on the senses, the Tibetan physician systematically examines a patient's urine in terms of its colour, sedimentation, odour, bubble formation and visible secretions. When urine is whisked in a white ceramic bowl, it reveals patterns and imagery from which a qualified doctor can arrive at a detailed analysis of the patient's state of health.

The origin of dreams

opposite

The central figure illustrates the formation of dream imagery from the subconscious mind (*alayavijyana*) located at the body's heart centre. During sleep the dream consciousness moves in conjunction with the life-sustaining breath. Moving up to the crown of the head, it creates images of the god realms and others such as ascending a mountain or a ladder. If the obscured consciousness descends to the lower body, the dreamer moves through dark, ominous landscapes. The surrounding panels illustrate omens encountered by the doctor on the way to the house of his patient, as well as dreams typical of individuals with a predominance of one or other of the three bodily humours.

Omens of death

below

According to Tibetan tradition, dreams influenced by the Lord of Death include those of riding on animals.

The nature of a patient's dreams can be analyzed in order to provide a supplementary form of diagnosis. Imbalances of Wind typically produce fragmentary dream images of flying or horse-riding. Those of Bile produce slow-moving dreamscapes featuring hues of red and yellow. The dreams of patients suffering from a predominance of Phlegm are often associated with physical contact and bliss, as well as white images such as snow, water, flowers and pearls. Certain dreams, such as those illustrated here, indicate the imminence of death.

Tibetan traditional belief holds that states of sleep and dream correspond to our experiences at the time of death when, after a period of unconsciousness, the mind, now freed of the physical body, begins to reawaken. According to Tibetan Buddhism, in this Bardo, or interim stage between one life and the next, the mind either recognizes its inherent luminosity or falls victim to a host of demonic projections.

opposite and below

Dream images portending death include riding on a fox or a human corpse, naked on a buffalo or camel, or (as pictured below) being swallowed by a giant fish. Similarly inauspicious are dreams of re-entering the womb, being swept away by water or sinking into a quagmire.

above

Dreams foretelling longevity and freedom from disease include riding on a horse or a bull, swimming across a river, travelling in a north-easterly direction, or escaping from dangerous circumstances.

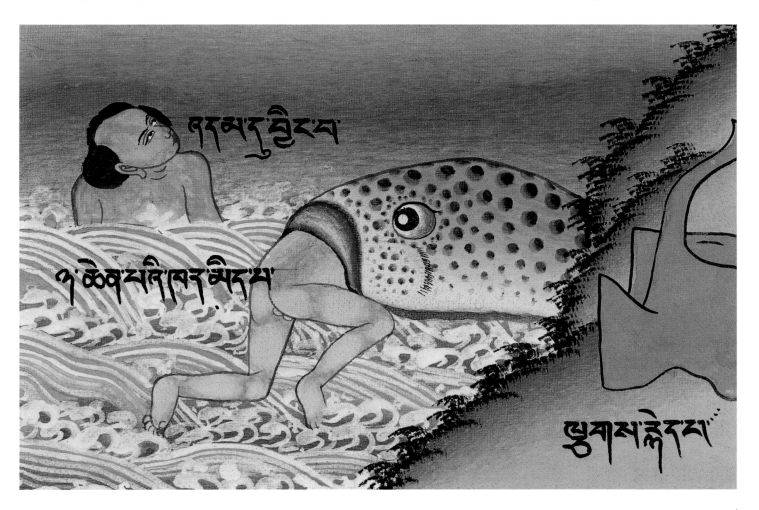

4 Healing: restoring balance

Perfect health, the cessation of all suffering, was the third Noble Truth taught by the Buddha over two thousand years ago. In Tibetan medicine *sowa rigpa*, or the science of healing, ranges from naturopathic health care to esoteric yogas that purify the body's inner essences, so eliminating the basis from which disease can arise. Unique to the Tibetan concept of healing is the Buddhist ideal of achieving liberation from the sufferings of conditioned existence. As Tibetan doctors claim, until ignorance and craving are removed from the mind-stream, no matter how healthy we may think we are, we are still ill. This primordial affliction of contracted awareness is capable of being cured only through the supreme elixir of spiritual practice. The esoteric health regimens of Tibetan medicine – from rejuvenation to sexual yogas – are all based on restoring the balance between body, heart and mind and removing the impediments to growth and spiritual awareness.

Tree of Healing Therapies

opposite

The Tree of Healing Therapies divides into four stems whose branches symbolize various aspects of Tibetan medical treatment. On the left, the stem of diet indicates the various types of foods that are recommended in cases of humoural imbalance. The stem of conduct divides into three branches and illustrates behaviour appropriate to patients suffering from imbalances of Wind, Bile or Phlegm. The fifteen branches of the third stem illustrate the tastes, potencies, tranquillizing and cathartic effects of a variety of medicines. The branch on the lower right reveals different methods of external therapy.

Preparing medicines

left

At the root of the Tree of Healing Therapies a group of doctors are engaged in preparing medicines. Tibetan physicians oversee, or personally conduct, every phase in the preparation of medicinal materials – from the initial stages of plant collection to the grinding, mixing and consecration of the resultant powders and pills. Many otherwise noxious natural substances, for example mercury, undergo elaborate purification processes to transform them into potent remedies.

Roots of treatment

The basis of the Tibetan medical system is to maintain balance between the psycho-physiological elements that constitute the human body. When pathology occurs, balance is restored through the systematic application of four divisions of healing therapies. The first approach is to introduce constructive changes in lifestyle and behaviour, including naturopathic therapies such as mineral baths and massage. Improper diet is viewed as a primary factor in the development of disease, and nutritional advice based on one's particular constitution is a central aspect of all treatment. The third approach is the prescription of natural remedies compounded from healing herbs and purified mineral essences. The fourth branch is that of external therapies, such as moxibustion, which is used to enhance the effect of herbal medicines.

Buddha and external therapies

opposite

Seated on a lotus throne, the Medicine Buddha is shown reabsorbing his wisdom emanation, 'Primordial Awareness' – the Buddha-form who expounded the original medical Tantras. The branch above and its three stems illustrate the use of external therapies in imbalanced conditions of the three humours. The branch to the upper right shows the curative effect of massage and moxibustion on patients with an imbalance of Wind. The branch below depicts bloodletting and bathing in waterfalls, recommended in cases of excess Bile. For imbalances of Phlegm two leaves illustrate the use of compresses and moxibustion.

Methods of treatment

left

As illustrated at the base of the Tree of Healing Therapies, in restoring wholeness and balance to the body's vital energies, Tibetan medicine relies on the syncretic application of the four roots: diet, conduct, internal medication and external therapy.

Paradigms of conduct

opposite

Illustrating the kinds of behaviour conducive to health as well as those which lead to disease, this thangka provides a synopsis of preventive health care. Beginning with examples of dangerous activities that jeopardize health and well-being, it goes on to illustrate healthy conduct specific to particular seasons. Also included are vignettes of beneficial religious activities, as well as conduct for prolonging the life span, such as taking alchemical elixirs made from precious minerals and plants.

Stages of intoxication

above and below

Although alcohol is recommended in the treatment of a variety of ailments, these images depict the consequences of excessive consumption. The first degree of drunkenness is described as 'shamelessness and lack of conscience' and the second degree 'resembles a rutting elephant'. The third degree is defined as 'prostrate mindlessness similar to a corpse'. Deepak Chopra has commented that 'Bad habits are just the worn-out ruts of the mind, paths that once led to freedom because they opened up new thoughts, but now lead nowhere.'

According to Tibetan medicine, the most important aspect of health care is recognizing which of our habits, even the ones we think are beneficial, actually lead to illness and suffering. Great emphasis is placed on preventive health practices, the most important of which is avoiding behaviour that endangers or depletes the life-force. As illustrated in this painting, these include hazardous pursuits such as riding untamed animals or wandering in dangerous places. Other harmful practices include conscious suppression of natural functions such as eating, sleeping or making love or, conversely, overindulgence – in which case what is normally beneficial becomes a cause of harm. At all phases of the healing process, Tibetan doctors emphasize the emergence from personal behaviour conditioned by ignorance, greed and aggression, as well as from the subtler faults of ego-clinging and spiritual complacency.

More than medicines, therapies or even diet, Tibetan medical teaching emphasizes preventive health care through behaviour that is alert to seasonal change and internal imbalances of the three humours. This sense of balance is symbolized above in the image of a man reclining 'on the borderline between sun and shade'. To maintain freedom from disease, the illustrations stress the proper observance of seasonal conduct, whether weeding fields, bathing in cooling waters or drinking medicinal wine. To prolong the life span and virility, the medical Tantras advocate practices of inner

alchemy, relying on supreme elixirs made from purified essences of mercury and gold, as well as the unequalled nectar of a qualified consort. Other practices regarded as conducive to health and long life (illustrated below) include massage, bathing in healing waters, and the weekly use of decoctions of yellow barberry to prevent diseases of the eyes. The essence of beneficial conduct, however, is based on intimate recognition of the interdependence of all life and understanding that only when our actions originate from a space of generosity, creativity and inner wholeness can true healing begin.

As food directly affects the body's three humours, or vital energies, proper diet is the basis of all Tibetan medical treatment. Foods with a warming quality, such as yak meat and sesame products, are recommended in conditions of cold disease, whereas foods with a cooling effect, such as beef and most grains, are emphasized in cases of excess heat. Foods are classified according to taste – sweet, sour, salty, bitter, and astringent – and are prescribed in the treatment of humoural imbalances.

Qualities of water

above

The best drinking water is said to be that collected from sunlit waterfalls; the worst is boiled water left standing for more than 24 hours.

Healing greens

below

Broth made from red goosefoot is used to cure disorders of all the humours; white dandelion is a remedy for diseases of the blood and Bile.

Life-sustaining food

below

Shown seated contentedly between a container of milk and a barrel of fresh meat broth, this figure illustrates the Tibetan concept of a healthy diet. Certain foods are credited with having especially tonic or healing properties. Fish, for example, is said to alleviate stomach ailments, improve eyesight and heal external sores; cooked nettles generate body heat and alleviate Wind disorders.

Balanced diet

above

Tibetan medicine recommends that at the conclusion of a meal the stomach be only three-quarters full, half with food, one quarter with liquids. The remaining quarter allows for the proper functioning of digestive enzymes. Certain food combinations, for example fish and eggs, are said to create toxic conditions within the body and to be harmful to health.

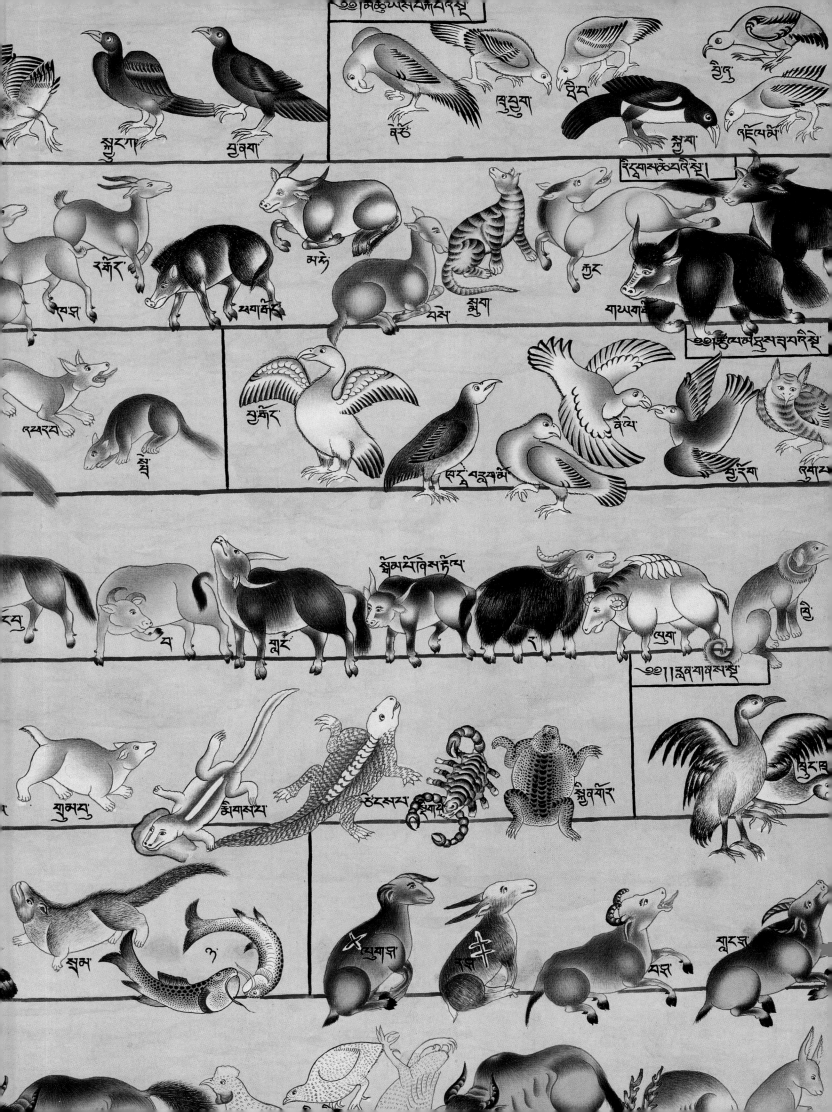

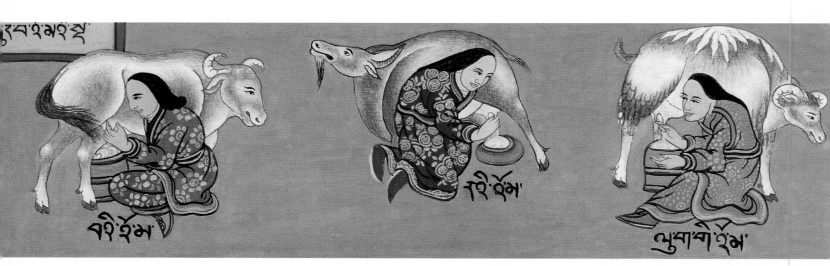

T he yak and its female counterpart the dri are the basis of
Tibetan pastoral life, and their products – milk, butter, meat
and hide – are the measure of all economic exchange. Along with
roasted barley flour and tea, milk and butter are the staples of
the Tibetan diet and are revered as supreme tonics. As Tsampa
Amchi stated, 'If food is the greatest medicine, the fresh milk of
the dri can be considered a kind of ambrosia. It heals all diseases
of the Wind, brings clarity to the complexion and peace and
composure to the mind.' Milk products also have spiritual
significance. Nomads begin each day by reciting prayers and

Types of milk

above

'Cow's milk counteracts diseases of
the lungs . . . cures cold disorders
and sharpens the intellect. Goat's
milk alleviates breathing disorders
and asthma. . . . Sheep's milk cures
disorders of Wind, but is harmful to
the heart and dulls the mind. The
milk of the dri increases virility, but
is harmful in disorders of Phlegm
and Bile. Horse's and donkey's milk
cures lung diseases, but clouds
discernment.'

From the Blue Beryl

offering milk to the unseen spirits of the land and sky. Their surplus butter is paid as tribute to the monasteries, where it is churned into butter tea for the monks and is used to fuel the myriad lamps lit in offering to the gods. Among nomads a barrel of milk is presented by a suitor to his prospective bride. Only if she drinks of it can their lives be joined in marriage. Milk is also a key ingredient in preparing the essence-extract elixirs used in Tantric rites of rejuvenation.

Milk as remedy

opposite below and below left

Tibetans attribute medicinal qualities to all milk and milk products. Boiling it half and half with water makes milk lighter and enhances its tonic effect. Transformed into yoghurt, it cures a variety of digestive complaints. Taken as whey, it loosens the stools and cleanses the channels. Milk reaches its supreme form, however, when churned into butter. As Dr Yeshe Donden maintains, 'Butter increases warmth, strength and life span. . . . It is very potent and has thousands of functions.'

Medicinal baths

ལུ་བཟེད

At auspicious times of the year, when the planet Venus shines in the morning sky, bathing outdoors is believed to cleanse not only the body, but to purify the mind-stream of accumulated karma. For diseases of the Bile and in hot summer weather, bathing in cool mountain streams is recommended.

Medicinal springs

below and opposite above

On the mythical Malaya mountain medicinal springs issue from fissures in the rocks. The five pools below are imbued with deposits of gold, silver, copper, iron and lead bitumen. The springs issuing from the calcite rocks above are described as nectar curative of diseases of the three humours. The limestone is of five varieties – 'male', 'boy', 'female', 'girl', and 'neuter' ('male' waters are prescribed for female patients and 'female' waters for ailing men).

The waters beneath the Himalayas and the Tibetan plateau erupt frequently in hot springs, which are revered as places of healing and rejuvenation. Many such natural spas have also become places of pilgrimage and spiritual retreat. Bathing in these sacred thermal springs is believed to purify both body and mind.

Taking the waters

below

To overcome the internal Wind that causes the body to age, Tibetan doctors advocate frequent bathing followed by regular massages with healing oils. Rubbing the body with sesame oil mixed with extracts of medicinal plants wards off disease, promotes longevity and increases both digestive fire and sexual stamina. In late winter and in spring, when an excess of Phlegm accumulates, Tibetans often use lentil flour instead of soap. Rubbing the dry flour on the body and then washing it off with water clears Phlegm from the system. To counteract imbalances of Bile and Wind, the Bath of Five Nectars is often prescribed; its chief ingredients are nutmeg and cloves, Tibetan tamarisk, juniper and dwarf rhododendron. To reap the full benefits of medicinal bathing, doctors claim, one should not bathe too often in a single day. To do so can result in imbalances of Wind.

Massage

Rejuvenating massage

left

Massage with medicated oils is said to slow the process of aging and increase vigour. Substances employed include melted butter mixed with nutmeg and aniseed, as well as animal fats such as otter and yak's tallow.

Therapeutic touch

below

The skilled masseuse can remove energy blockages in the subtle body. Lengthwise strokes are used to release tensions and accumulated toxins. Circular strokes are said to charge the body with healing energy. Massage is used to treat a variety of stress-related disorders, as well as in cases of neuralgia, multiple sclerosis, cardio-vascular diseases and pinched nerves.

Combining the use of seventy-eight specific acupressure points with the medicinal effects of oils and plant extracts, Tibetan massage is used in a variety of contexts to overcome disease and enhance the life-force. As the skin is the juncture between the external environment and the pathways of subtle consciousness that run the length of the body, massage is used in Tibetan medicine to produce a positive influence not only on physical health, but on consciousness itself. Unique to Tibetan massage is the use of chickpea flour at the conclusion of a session to absorb excess oils and counteract any side-effects resulting from increased secretions of the body's mucous membranes.

Massage in winter

above and right
....
In the cold season, when the body's
internal metabolism is most active,
Tibetan doctors recommend massage
with warm eaglewood and sesame oil,
bone marrow, or melted butter with
musk and extracts of medicinal herbs.
In order to satisfy the body's need
for increased nutrition, massage is
supplemented by a diet of rich and
oily foods, including broth made
from fresh meat.

Sexual health

According to Dr Lobsang Dolma, 'a man's sexual organs have a certain energy field, and so do a woman's. When man and woman unite, these energy fields harmonize perfectly.' In Tibetan medicine, sexual prohibitions refer ultimately to the obsessive cravings and divisive desires that obscure the healing powers of pure sensuality. Only when it is free of dissipating passions can sexuality emerge as a vital force of unbounded creativity, the spontaneous expression of compassion and delight.

Sexual conduct

below
According to the medical Tantras, the following practices can be harmful to health: Intercourse with dissimilar species, with the wife of another man or with a woman of unpleasant disposition. Sex during menstruation or pregnancy is also considered to be injurious, as is homo-eroticism and excessive loss of semen and vital fluids.

Remedies for insomnia

left

To cure insomnia Tibetan doctors
recommend that hot milk be drunk
in the middle of the day and wine
and meat broth in the evening.
Massaging the head with sesame oil
and administering warm ear-drops
made from freshly melted butter
mixed with musk are also considered
highly effective techniques for relaxing
the mind and inducing sleep.

Combating drowsiness

below

The need for excessive amounts of
sleep is a symptom associated with
the accumulation of toxins caused by
improper combinations of food, as
well as stagnant energies resulting
from sedentary habits and lack of
exercise. To correct these imbalances,
Tibetan doctors recommend emetic
medicines and fasting to detoxify the
system, and increased sexual activity
to stimulate the body's vital forces.

The medical Tantras specify particular rules pertaining to sleep.
In spring a short period of sleep after lunch helps avoid Wind
disorders. In autumn, winter or summer sleep during the daytime
increases Phlegm, and body and mind will become heavy, with
a tendency to develop headaches, colds and contagious fevers.

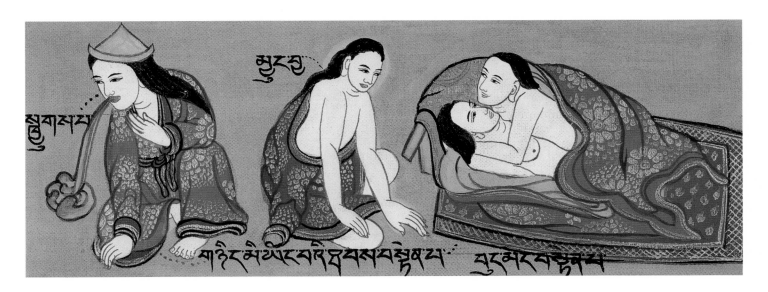

By examining a patient's pulse and urine and inquiring closely
into the nature of his symptoms, the Tibetan physician looks deeply
into his underlying state of health. Like the Lama who guides his
disciples into a recognition of the unbounded openness at the heart
of all existence, the physician in the Tibetan
medical system exemplifies the Buddhist ideal
of liberating beings from their largely self-
imposed distress. As Trogawa Rinpoche said,
Tibetan doctors are trained to recognize the
emotional and psychological disorders that are
often manifested in physical symptoms. 'That
means not just prescribing medicines but
helping a patient discover ways of restoring
balance in his activities, diet and ways of
thinking.' In Tibetan medicine healing is more

The benevolent healer

above and below
The physician dispelling fear and
anxiety, and prescribing medicines.

than a mere matter of overcoming disease: it concerns the
primordial unrest that underlies all imbalances of mind and body.
Only once the patient directs himself to a goal larger than his own
well-being can he ever transcend his deepest afflictions. This is
theiparadox of healing that Buddhism presents: if we truly aspire
to wholeness in body, mind and spirit, we must emerge decisively

from our own sufferings and embrace those of others. When we
live on behalf of all beings, Tibetan doctors maintain, transient
illnesses are largely self-correcting. It is for this reason, Sangwa
Rinpoche said, that the Buddha himself knowingly ate the tainted
meat that was to lead to his death – not to teach by example how
 to die with equanimity, but how to live in the abundance of
selfless compassion.

Severing the roots of illness

above

In a series of metaphorical vignettes,
the holder of the lineage of the Four
Tantras is shown severing with a
sword the untimely noose of death,
shattering with a hammer the nails of
acute disease and, with an iron hook,
extracting patients from the swamp
of suffering.

Tibetan doctors advise taking emetic medicines in spring to purge the body of Phlegm, and in summer to purify the body of accumulated Wind disorders; in autumn special purgatives are used to clear excess Bile accumulated over the summer.

Cathartics

right

Purgatives and emetics are administered in the early stages of fever and in cases of acute poisoning, gastritis, rheumatism, dropsy, parasites, defective vision and diseases of Bile. Principal plant ingredients for purgatives include chebulic myrobalan, croton, madder grass and spurge. Standard emetics include mountain sorrel, thistle, spurge and narrow-leaved sweetflag.

Monk-physicians administering enemas

opposite above and below, and below

Enemas prepared from medicinal substances are recommended for use in treating cases of abdominal distention, epigastric tumours, diarrhoea, depletion of generative fluid, parasites and general debility resulting from disorders of Wind.

Bloodletting and external therapy

ব্থুর'ট্রীন্'থা

Bloodletting

left and below

To restore balance to the organism and rid it of excess heat, bloodletting is performed in specific cases of fever, gout, wounds, ulcers, blood disorders and leprosy. In general, bloodletting is not recommended for the treatment of patients under sixteen or for those over seventy.

Bloodletting channels

opposite

To separate pure and impure blood, preparations for bloodletting include the administering of decoctions of either moonseed or the three kinds of myrobalan fruit. Tourniquets are then applied to different parts of the patient's body. Once the blood vessels are bound, bloodletting is performed directly on the superficial veins at precise points along their pathways. At the conclusion of the bloodletting, moxa is applied to the incised points except for those located on the neck. The lower panels of this thangka illustrate various indications for the application of moxa.

Whereupon medicine, dietary and behavioural modification, together with the milder forms of external therapy such as massage, prove insufficient in removing the cause of disease, Tibetan physicians resort to more invasive therapies including bloodletting, moxibustion and minor surgery. Using up to seventy-nine specific points on the body, bloodletting is performed to dissipate excess heat and cure dysfunctions of blood and Bile corresponding in Chinese medicine to excess Yang. In present-day Tibetan medicine bloodletting is rarely practised, though moxibustion and the traditional Tibetan form of acupuncture are still common procedures.

মান্ন্'ন্র্যা

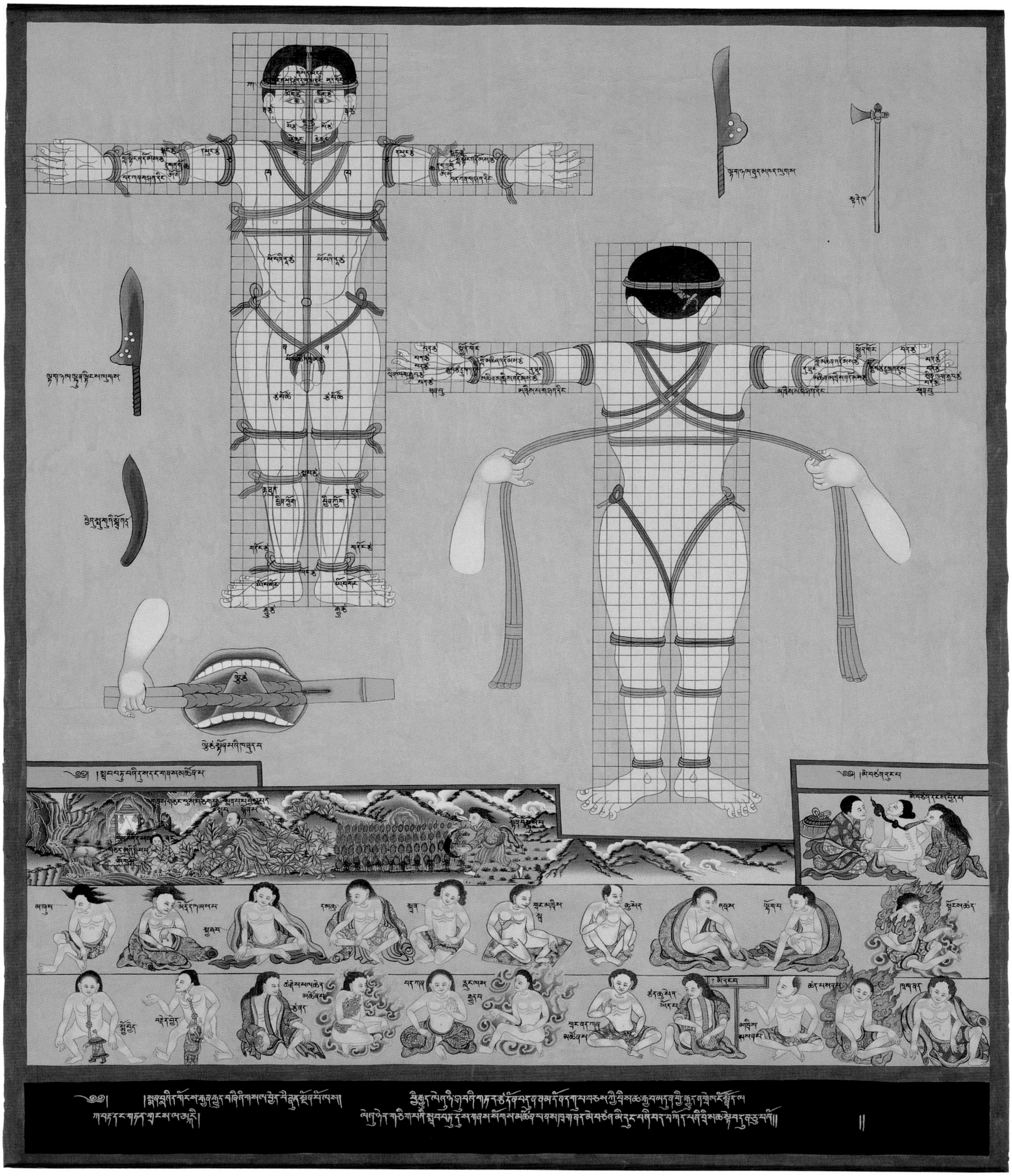

Whereas bloodletting is used in diseases associated with
excessive heat, the Tibetan practice of moxibustion – in which
herbs are burned directly on specific points on the skin – is used
to mollify cold disorders and tonify the system. Unlike the more
familiar form of moxibustion practised in China, which relies
almost exclusively on artemisia, Tibetans use a variety of medicinal
herbs, including gerbera, yellow champa, nutmeg, saffron, chebulic
myrobalan, ginger and thistle, depending on the specific nature
of the illness. Moxibustion was particularly popular in the colder
regions of northern Tibet, where it was widely practised, almost
to the exclusion of other forms of therapy. Strangely, the Tibetan
medical paintings contain no illustrations of the unique form of
acupuncture called 'golden needle' therapy, which is thought to
have originated in Tibet and entered China via Mongolia.

Collecting moxa plants

above

For maximum efficacy healing plants –
in this case gerbera leaves to be used
in moxibustion – should be gathered
in the autumn during the period of the
waxing moon, the collecting process
to be carried out by an innocent child
under the direction of the physician.

Administering moxa

opposite

Small cones or flat pellets made of
gerbera and other herbs are ignited
at several of 71 specific points on the
patient's body. Moxibustion is
considered especially useful in cases
of indigestion, morbid pallor, dropsy,
internal tumours, muscular spasms,
fever, epilepsy and madness.

overleaf
....
Two thangkas illustrating the points on the body
associated with techniques of bloodletting,
moxibustion and minor surgery, differentiated,
respectively, by the use of the colours blue, yellow
and red.

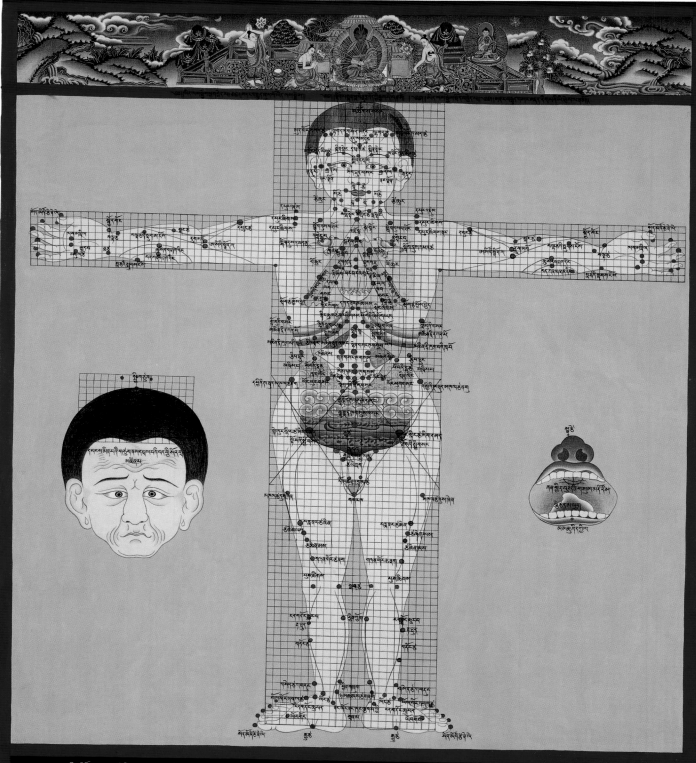

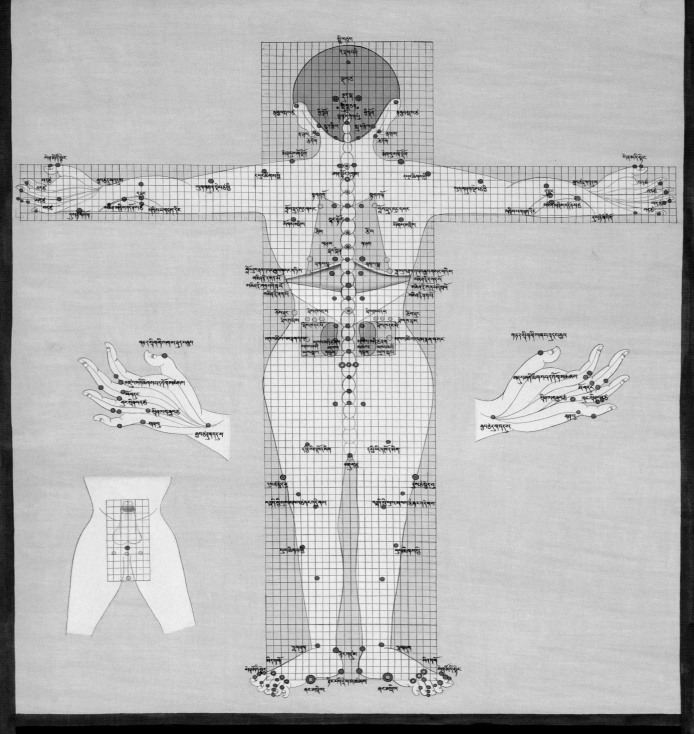

Nasal cathartics

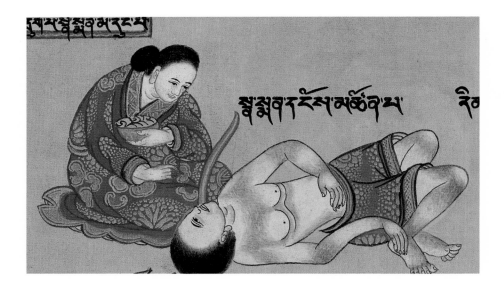

 དྲེ་ར་སྦྱིན་ཚུལ་གསང་བ།

སྣ་སྨན་རྡོས་མཆོན་པ།   ནི

Administering snuff

left and below
Nasal medications, administered
either as powders or drops, are
indicated in chronic sinus disorders,
acute angina, conjunctivitis, diseases
of the ears and brain, and diffusion of
the blood vessels caused by cranial
fractures. The ingredients include
honey, powdered strawberry leaves,
sea salt, narrow-leaved sweetflag,
costus, licorice, white aconite,
soapwort and galangal.

Five distinct diseases of the nose are attributed to inappropriate
diet and behaviour, as well as the influences of harmful spirits.
To cure ailments ranging from abscesses to excess Phlegm, nasal
cathartics are prepared from a variety of medicinal substances.

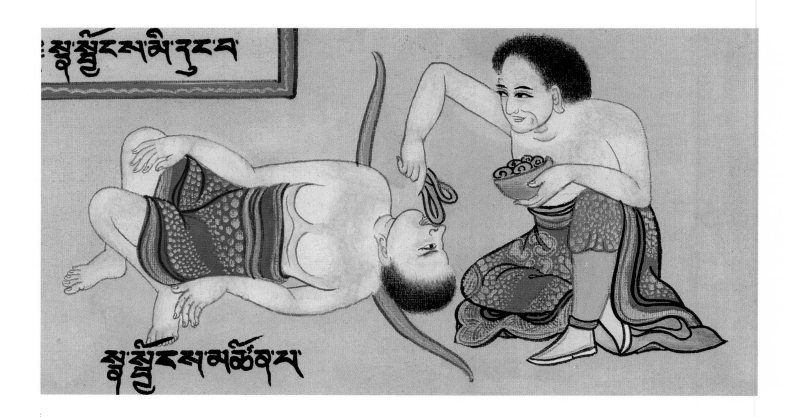

སྣ་སྦྱོར་ས་མི་དུར་བ།

སྣ་སྦྱུ་ར་ས་མཆོན་པ།

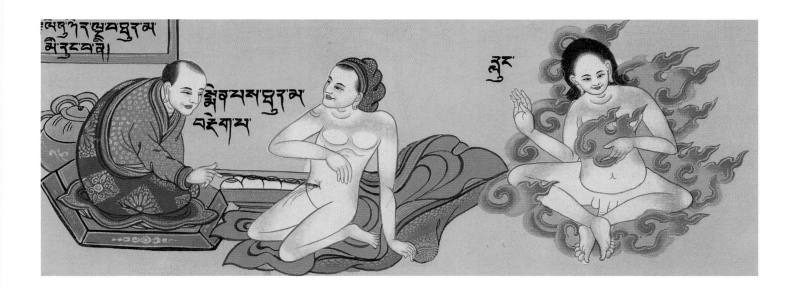

External therapies in Tibetan medicine range from applications of pharmaceutically prepared ointments to cauterization and pus extraction by sucking pathogenic material out of the body with the aid of a yak's horn. Although surgery was practised in early Tibet, it was prohibited after the failure of a heart operation carried out on the mother of a ninth-century king. To this day Tibetans avoid resorting to the use of surgery in all except the most drastic of circumstances, believing that such intervention causes irreparable damage to the body's life-force.

Performing minor surgery

above

Although the practice is rare today, the medical Tantras specify 110 points where either a cold or heated stylet can be used to drain pathological fluids from tumours, goitres and assorted swellings.

Applying ointments

right

Ointments prepared from animal fats, butter or vegetable oil are mixed with herbs and used to treat ailments including coarse skin, deficiency of blood or reproductive fluids, nervous tension, poor eyesight and disorders of Wind.

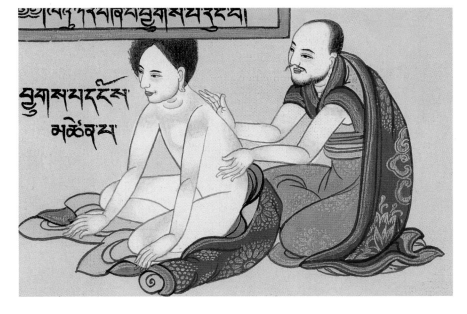

W hen the body's humours are imbalanced, disease arises.
When they flow dynamically, there is health. Of the three humours,
Wind is the most important as it maintains the symbiotic
relationship between the heat of Bile and the fluid energy of
Phlegm. Wind is also the vital force most subject to imbalance,
leading to symptoms such as shortness of breath, dizziness,
weakness, depression and anxiety. These two panels outline a
concise regimen for the treatment of imbalanced Wind. Diet

above

Various dietary items recommended
in the treatment of Wind disorders.

should be adjusted to include heavy, warming foods such as sesame oil, wine, molasses, aged butter, mutton, the flesh of marmots, horses, donkeys and human beings, garlic and onion. Conduct should involve staying in warm places, getting sufficient sleep and wearing warm clothing. External therapy for Wind disorders includes mild enemas of old butter, oily compresses, and moxibustion on the crown of the head. To counteract overactivity of the air element, medicines for Wind imbalances are compounded primarily from the earth element and are strong and pungent.

Gathering herbs

The identification and gathering of medicinal plants and herbs constitutes an essential part of a Tibetan doctor's training. The various components used in the preparation of healing remedies are collected at different seasons – fruits in autumn, leaves during the summer months, branches and barks during the spring and roots in winter. Mantras and invocations of the healing Buddha are often recited during the time of actual collection, after which the herbs are carefully cleaned, dried and in some cases detoxified, before being prepared for use as medicines.

The rainy season

below
....
According to the medical Tantras, the leaves, sap and shoots of medicinal plants should be collected during the rainy season, when their leaves are fully developed.

Collecting aconite

above right
....
Diseases of heat are relieved by the tips of aconite grown in shady places; conversely, cold diseases are relieved by the roots of aconite that has grown in the sun.

Herbs in autumn

below
The flowers and fruits of healing plants
should be harvested during autumn.

Plant medicines

The snow-swept mountains of central Tibet and the lush forests in the eastern and southern districts contain a vast wealth of plants with healing properties. The Tibetan materia medica lists more than a thousand known medicinal herbs, but the medical Tantras also assert that there is not a single substance existing in nature that, once its properties are identified, cannot be used in some way to cure disease. In describing her training as a Tibetan doctor in the Himalayan valley of Kyirong, Dr Lobsang Dolma commented that 'For every single herb we could identify and

Materia medica

below
Ten of the thangkas illustrating the Blue Beryl are devoted to healing plants; they describe the medicinal action of over 500 herbs, flowers, grasses and roots. The first panel below begins with henbane, which is used to treat parasites, and ends with two varieties of ginseng. The second panel depicts four types of sedge, Chinese basil and horned cumin used to alleviate contagious fever. The third panel includes cobra lily, bulrush, strawberry and fenugreek; the latter used to cure diarrhoea and diseases of the lungs.

whose medicinal properties we could correctly assess, there were
a hundred more herbs that we knew nothing about. . . . We felt
a deep humility in front of Nature's treasures.'

The most precious of all plants in the Tibetan pharmacopoeia,
Aruranamgyal (*Terminalia chebula*, shown on the right), is used
not only as a cure for innumerable diseases, but its fruits are
regarded as a supreme tonic with the power to bestow happiness
and well-being. It is a sprig of the revered myrobalan tree that
the Medicine Buddha is shown holding in his outstretched hand.

Preparing remedies

I̶n the Tibetan system of compounding remedies, herbs are combined with minerals, jewels and precious stones, as well as with substances of animal origin. Medicinal effect is ensured not only by the presence of particular ingredients, but through specific combinations and methods of potentization. Remedies in the form of pills, incense and medicated oils commonly contain up to fifty or more different ingredients. Prayers and mantras are recited to imbue the remedies with additional potency.

Gemstones and minerals

opposite

Substances such as gold, silver, ruby, turquoise and coral are considered some of the most powerful ingredients in Tibetan medicine and form the basis of the seven types of *rinchen rilbus*, or 'Precious Pills', which are used to prevent and cure a diversity of life-threatening ailments.

Preparing remedies

above and right

Medicines are compounded as powders, pills and pastes. To ensure the potency of a compound, at all phases in the preparation, the doctor's purity of intention is considered just as important as his knowledge of proportions and technique.

Mythical origin of bezoars

above

Medicinal concretions found in the stomachs of elephants, frogs, geese, vultures, snakes, peacocks, bears and pigeons are said to have originated from an elixir of precious gems thrown into the sea.

Exotic remedies

opposite

This thangka features a variety of exotic ingredients used in medicines, for example: the purified seminal essences of male and female yogins; the earth from an ant's nest; scorched human hair; vaginal secretions at the time of orgasm; scabs of smallpox pustules; earth dug from beneath the drainage channel of a house or from a north-facing cave.

Musk and bear bile

right

The aromatic glands from musk deer are said to act as antidotes to poisons and to be beneficial in disorders of the kidneys and liver. Bear bile halts necrosis and is used to treat diseases of the eyes.

Although the majority of substances used in medicines are of plant and mineral origin, animal products comprise a significant minority. Deer horn, elephant liver, bear bile, the urine of red cows, as well as substances derived from humans, were all traditionally employed, despite Buddhist injunctions against killing for human profit. Medicines from animal sources are purified thoroughly before use, such as the backbone of yaks, which are crushed and mixed with gold to make a powerful female contraceptive.

Whether chemical analysis shows them to be placebos or panaceas, healing substances are those which inspire wholeness and rouse us from stagnant patterns of thought and awareness. According to the Tibetan medical Tantras, all things in nature are a potential source of healing. Even urine and blood, when purified, can have vitalizing effects on the organism from which they derive. The ultimate remedies, however, are the body's subtle essences and glandular secretions, purified and transformed through meditation and Tantric yoga.

Medicinal bones

above

Bones of various species are useful in curing complaints as diverse as muscular spasms, heart disease, and colic. Pictured at the far right, the bones of a human being killed by lightning are said to cure dysentery.

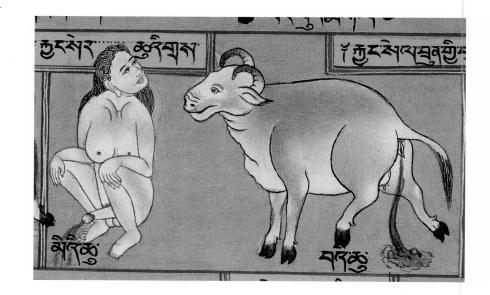

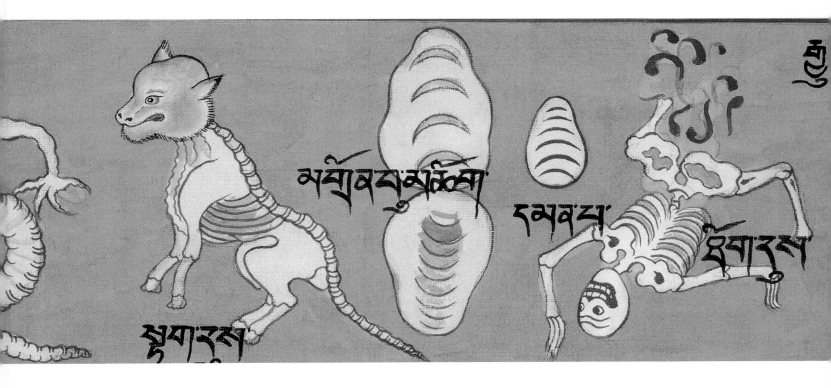

Urine as remedy

opposite below

A patient's own urine is prescribed as a readily available remedy for septic disorders and flu. As suggested in recent German research, autogenous solutions of one's own urine and blood can rejuvenative the immune system and have a positive influence in a variety of chronic diseases.

Cannibalism for medicinal purposes

below

Various parts of the human body can be consumed to cure contagious fevers, poisoning, Bile disorders and protracted labour. Whether contemplated or consumed, skeletons symbolize a wholesome awareness of the truth that lies behind appearances.

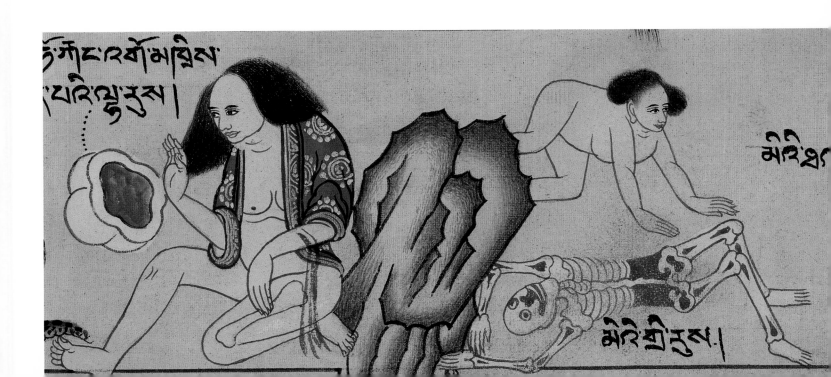

Healing through ritual

Tibetan medicine maintains that certain illnesses are curable only by elaborate rituals performed by Lamas, yogis, or shamanic healers. As Dr Lobsang Dolma stated, 'In cases of diseases caused by evil spirits, medicines will effect a temporary cure, but the illness will always return.' Tibetan rites of healing – synthesizing medicine, magic and spirituality – redirect the mind and body to a state of integration.

Lhamo, a Tibetan spirit medium in Kathmandu, attributes most disease to malevolent energies that obstruct awareness. Healings

Prayers and rhythmic drumming help to ease mind and body into a state of balance. Tibetan rites of healing reshape our experience of reality and exorcise the fears and fixed beliefs that produce patterns of anxiety and illness. When the mind is restored to its natural state, spirits of agitation, doubt and confusion lose their capacity to unbalance the emotions and inflict disease.

occur through her sudden revelations of the underlying affliction and cathartic treatments in which physical substances are sucked from the patient's body. By coercing renegade energies of mind and body into new and beneficent patterns, shamanic rites are often as effective as they are inexplicable. Lhamo, in her state of trance, sees deeply into her patients' inner condition. Liberation from suffering requires an equal act of faith: the optimism necessary to recognize in every moment the possibility of spontaneous healing.

Inextricably linked to Buddhist philosophy, the Tibetan art of healing posits ignorance of the interconnectedness of life as the primal cause of suffering. Similarly, the attainment of wisdom and compassion is upheld as the ultimate goal of all healing. As

Deceiving death

above and left

In pre-Buddhist shamanic practices, a patient's life-force is reclaimed through the subjugation and ritual appeasement of disease-causing entities. Thread crosses, magical daggers, symbolic effigies, prayers and invocations are all used to convert demonic energies into forces of healing. One of the most powerful methods was the ransoming of the patient's life by freeing animals otherwise destined for slaughter; this is evidence of the recognition that compassion and generosity, not fear and coercion, are the forces that activate the process of healing.

Sogyal Rinpoche said, 'To cure our most fundamental disease –
primordial ignorance – there is no medicine besides the wisdom
arising from meditation. Only through realizing our true nature
can we hope to bring lasting benefit to ourselves or others.' In the
healing practices of Tibetan medicine the inert and unknowing
energies that unbalance our lives are restored to conscious
awareness. Healing is to make whole, to unify, to eroticize. In
recognizing our inseparability from all life, we may discover
wholeness and healing, not simply in turning away from the
world, but in living more abundantly in a spirit of generosity
and unbounded play.

Empowering the life-force

below

In Tibetan culture, the act of freeing
birds, fish and other beings from
captivity or imminent death is believed
to have a reciprocal benefit on one's
own life-force. Representing more
than a perfunctory observance of the
Buddhist ideal of compassion, such
acts express the generosity and
creativity at the heart of all existence.
In the act of restoring wholeness,
Buddhists claim, one renews both
self and other. Tibetan art has an
analogous function. It frees us from
accustomed perception. Here the
Buddhist ideal is shown not as a
'fisher of men', but as one who opens
the nets of ignorance and partiality
and restores beings to their naturally
liberated state.

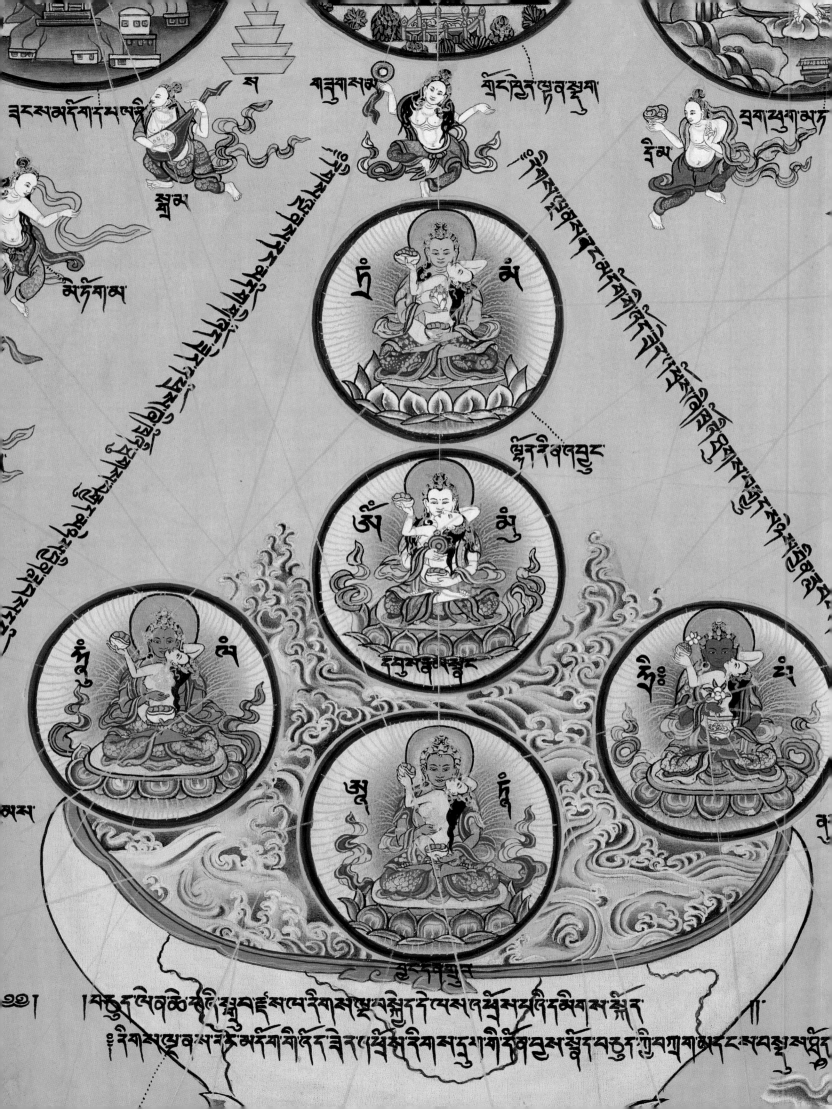

5 Liberation: awakening the body of light

The ultimate goal of Tibetan medicine is not only to restore body and mind to a state of health and internal balance, but to remove the subtle physical and mental defilements that obscure our inner Buddha Nature. To untie the knots of karmic conditioning and free the mind of self-limiting patterns of thought and experience, Tibetan medicine relies on the inner yogas and meditation practices of Tantric Buddhism. Enhanced by medicinal extracts and empowered substances, Tantric sadhanas transform ordinary experiences of pleasure and pain into radiant awareness of our innermost being. As the Tantras proclaim, 'Great wisdom dwells within the body', and Tibetan doctors continually profess that the bliss which arises from within is the only medicine that can cure the ailment from which all others arise – ignorance of our own true nature.

The Buddha revealed how disease and the contemplation of suffering can enlarge our sympathies, motivate us on the spiritual path, and ultimately free us from compulsive behaviour based on ignorance, greed and aggression. Full integration of the physical, emotional and spiritual currents that define human existence depends, however, on the inner union of the body's 'solar' and 'lunar', or male and female, energies. In this process of psycho-physical transformation the body's innermost essence is revealed as the inseparability of wisdom and luminosity. The Buddha's Fourth Noble Truth – the path of liberation from all sufferings of body and mind – is the ultimate panacea, pointing directly to the bliss and incandescence of our innermost being.

Yogin

above

Spiritual practice transforms the discordant energies of mind and body into radiant clarity. Blowing on a thigh-bone trumpet, a Tantric yogin celebrates liberation from all behaviour conditioned by fear, greed and attachment.

Buddhas with consorts

opposite

In spheres of rainbow light representing the transmuted essence of the body's most subtle energies, the five Dhyani Buddhas in union with their consorts direct us towards awareness of the 'inner mandala' – the body's blissful currents of 'male' and 'female' energies which, when unified through meditation, give rise to the wisdom and compassion of the enlightened mind.

Suffering and discontent are the first contemplations on the Buddhist path. Recognizing how petty sentiments and rigid beliefs constrict our lives, the mind aspires to more inclusive awareness. The aspiration to penetrate to the very essence of life and death comes only when one tires of conventional attitudes and preoccupations. As Lama Sangwa stated, 'Even illness is precious, as it teaches us the transience of all existence . . . Make use of this body now and recognize the Buddha within!'

Meditation and study

above

'Cutting through the limits of intellect, the mind's natural radiance spontaneously manifests itself. Without philosophizing, without clinging or grasping, look into the essence of the self-manifesting Buddha-Mind!'

Tantra of the Secret Lamp

Practising generosity

above

'Whatever joy there is in this world
Comes from desiring the happiness of
    others.
Whatever suffering there is . . .
Comes from desiring happiness for
    oneself . . .
What need is there to say much more?
The childish work for their own
    benefit;
The Buddhas work for the benefit of
    others.
Just look at the difference between
    them!'

Shantideva

Requesting the teachings

left

The Buddhist teachings of Tibet were
transmitted by ordained monks and
lamas, as well as by white-robed
Tantric yogins whose activities were
independent of formal monastic life.

Initiation and empowerment

Before practising the Tantric yogas that reveal the mind's inherent radiance, mind and body are matured through initiation. Four sequential empowerments, each associated with progressive levels of subtlety and bliss, activate the practitioner's inner mandala of energy-channels and psychic nerves. Purifying the mind stream of subtle obscurations, initiation is not always through formal rites, but often arises through potent existential encounters. The great siddha Khyungpo Naljor, for example, realized the nature of mind when the dakini Niguma offered him a skull-cup full of ambrosial water and pointed a finger at his heart. Tsele Natsok Rangdrol, a seventeenth-century poet, philosopher and meditation master, declared that 'Empowerment is the king of all methods that cause the original wisdom inherent in yourself to manifest itself naturally.'

Transmission of the Tantras

opposite

The final painting illustrating the Tibetan medical Tantras concerns the transmission of the science of healing, which has as its ultimate goal the complete emancipation of body, mind and spirit. The fully realized physician is shown attaining Buddhahood in a body of light.

Strengthening the life-force

below

Opening the way to spiritual energy through gestures of humility, a patient receives the empowerment of longevity. Certain Tantric initiations were given not only to practitioners, but to purify the karmic tendencies and enhance the lives of ordinary beings.

Deity yoga

opposite

Visualizing oneself in the archetypal form of a Tantric deity, body, mind and spirit aspire to a universal ideal of enlightened awareness. As expressions of the radiance and bliss at the core of all beings, deities are emanated and reabsorbed into light from the practitioner's heart centre. In this painting the physician wields a *vajra* sceptre mirroring the form of the deity Vajrapani who appears on the thangka above him. When viewed with openness and understanding, Tibetan art leads us to identify with images that reflect our innermost nature – a space of infinite creative potential.

The healing Buddha

right

The Buddha of healing herbs – the king of physicians – who expounds the medical Tantras is revealed through meditation as inseparable from our own innermost nature; the healing qualities of wisdom and compassion are expressions of the self-manifesting radiance at the heart of all existence. The Bardo Thodel, a meditation text that is said to liberate upon being heard, states:

'This mind of yours is emptiness and
    luminosity
inseparably conjoined.
Without birth or death, it is the
    Buddha of immortal light . . .
When you recognize the pristine
    nature of your mind
as no other than the Buddha
Looking into your own mind is resting
    in the mind of the Buddha.'

Lf initiation bestows the seed of liberation, it is spiritual practice that brings it to fruition. Just as medical theory remains abstract unless it is applied, so too are concepts of enlightenment unless realized within our own body and mind. In Tibetan tradition, the wisdom that arises from meditation is upheld as the greatest medicine, for it alone dispels the deluded conceptions that imprison us in the world of suffering.

Buddhism offers infinite approaches to overcoming the forces of ignorance, greed and aggression that obscure our innermost potential. At the heart of all paths, however, lies the simple recognition that from the very beginning our own individual nature is no different from that of the Buddhas.

Buddha Nature is the natural condition of mind and body purified of their habitual obscurations. Whether understood as a seed potential or a reality fully present yet temporarily veiled, Buddha Nature is the premise, path and final result of Buddhist practice and the foundation of the Tibetan medical sciences. Buddha Nature is the dynamic responsiveness of our innermost being to a world suffused with suffering and pain. The healing qualities of wisdom and compassion are the natural attributes of the awakened mind which sees spontaneously the openness and interconnectedness of all phenomena. Buddha Nature, as no other than our own intrinsic awareness, awakens us to our true potential. According to Lama Shabkar, 'This ordinary mind, unfabricated and natural, is the expansive Buddha mind free from limitations. Through the efforts of analyzing and cultivating, you will never perceive its essential nature.' Once recognized, the mind's intrinsic radiance expresses itself without bounds to restore all beings to a state of wholeness and exaltation.

In Tantrism, Buddha Nature expresses itself dynamically in the form of archetypal deities embodying innate human potential. To overcome self-limiting concepts and perceptions, the practitioner identifies himself with a particular deity with whom he feels karmic resonance. Generated from the practitioner's heart centre, the *yidam* represents the selflessness and power of our innermost being. Through the enlightened intention embodied by the *yidam*, we discover that mind itself is the absolute deity, the true Buddha. Resting in the natural radiance of our own Buddha mind, all attachment and subtle clinging dissolves in the nature of self-manifesting light.

Icons of awakened energy

opposite

Expressing the dynamic energy of enlightened mind, the deity Hayagriva arises from primal space in an aureole of fire, wrapped in animal pelts and garlanded with bone ornaments and severed heads. Blazing through contracted states of hesitancy and insecurity, Hayagriva tramples on human figures representing egocentric concepts of self and personality. In the consecration of Tibetan medicines and rejuvenating elixirs, the physician visualizes himself as Hayagriva, empowering medicinal substances with the potency to heal and transform. Referred to as the 'protector of the elixir', Hayagriva represents the transmuted energy of aggression and wrath converted to all-accomplishing wisdom. To benefit beings, Buddha Nature takes an infinite variety of forms; yet, as the fourteenth-century meditation master Longchen Rabjam declared, 'For the Buddhahood which is totally and naturally pure, do not search anywhere but in your own mind. . . . In the self-liberated state of our essential being all that arises is the magical display of Intrinsic Awareness.'

The greater elixir of rejuvenation

opposite

An inverted skull-cup filled with ambrosial nectar, the 'greater elixir of rejuvenation', refers to empowered substances which purify the body's subtle-energy channels, restore vigour and confer long life. The various light spheres shown emanating from deities and bodhisattvas are representations of the visualizations performed in conjunction with the empowerment of the elixir. In its purest form the practices of inner alchemy represent the perennial quest for the immortal condition of the Buddhas.

Preparing nectar-elixir

below

Rituals and meditation are features of the preparation of the elixirs which bestow long life. Red and white seminal fluids representing the essence of enlightened mind, or transformed desire, are visualized as flowing down from the Buddhas and their consorts, merging into the bowl of medicine and consecrating its contents as the nectar of immortality.

Tibetan medical theory holds that the impurities within our bodies, left as the residue of delusion, greed and aggression, cloud awareness and obscure our full potential. The Tibetan science of rejuvenation is based on the practices of the Indian Mahasiddhas, many of whom practised forms of inner alchemy to purify the body's subtle-energy currents and prepare it as a vessel of transformation. The lesser goal of restoring health and prolonging the life span was not overlooked, and many of the Tibetan practices of rejuvenation are said to lead to dramatic physical changes, such as grey hair returning to its natural colour, and the achievement of extreme longevity. Such rejuvenation practices are often performed on retreat in conjunction with meditation. One lama described a Tibetan yogini who had subsisted for decades solely on the subtle extracts of flowers. Rejuvenation techniques serve not only to purify the body of disease and restore youthful qualities, but remove the defilements of consciousness that obscure our underlying Buddha Nature.

Nectar-elixir

left

The alchemical substances used in rites and practices conferring longevity are prepared in accordance with elaborate rituals. According to Dr Yeshi Donden, 'If the medicine is prepared well, signs of success emerge: the body becomes younger, white hair turns black again, and even new teeth can develop. When such signs appear, you have succeeded, and it is not necessary to take more.'

Cleansing impurities

below

For the nectar-elixir to be effective the body must first be cleansed of all impurities. This panel illustrates some of the ingredients used for internal purification. Bowls containing the three fruits of chebulic, belleric and embellic myrobalan are followed by rock salt, longpepper, ginger, white sweet flag, turmeric, false black pepper and molasses. In order to achieve the greatest efficacy these ingredients should be mixed with the urine of a red cow.

To realize the full potential of the human body, the Tibetan healing tradition developed formulas for rejuvenating the cells and purifying the subtle essences within it. Some of the substances used, such as mercury, are toxic in an unrefined state. Other ingredients include precious metals and gemstones such as gold and diamonds. Dr Trogawa has noted, however, that the potency of the elixirs is derived from the rituals of consecration as much as from the substances themselves. Some of the most powerful essence-extracts are prepared from fluids drawn from flowers. Tibet abounds with accounts of great meditators who for years consumed nothing but flower extracts and water.

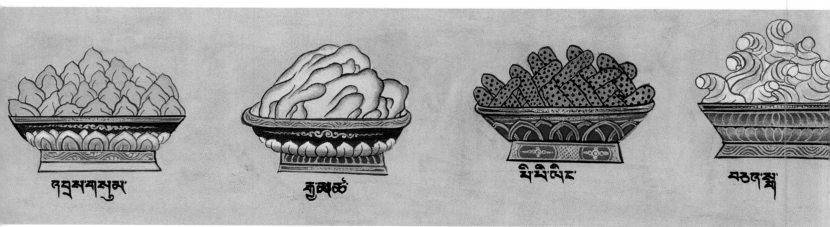

Recent research suggests that some of the Buddhist siddhas of ancient India may have used the fungus *Amanita muscaria* and other psychotropic substances in their alchemical formulas. Texts associated with pilgrimage sites in the Tibetan borderlands describe magical plants that 'bestow the eight siddhis and cause one to remember past lives'. The ultimate transformative elixirs, however, are found within the body itself. The *tigles*, the refined essences of the body's most subtle energies, and bio-chemical secretions, such as beta-carbolines released from the pineal gland during advanced practices of Tantric yoga, are the self-manifesting elixirs which transform the life force without being dependent on external substances.

Essence extracts

above

The medical Tantras list numerous preparations that can be used to promote longevity. For individuals with a predominance of Bile, the supreme elixir is prepared from the refined essences of gold, silver, copper, iron and mercury. For those with a predominance of Phlegm, the use of capsicum mixed with butter and honey is recommended. A third variety based on the three myrobalan fruits is said to remove illnesses of the three humours, sharpen the senses, and suspend the process of aging.

In the rites of rejuvenation the practitioner visualizes both himself and the medicine in the form of deities. Reciting mantras, he imagines that the medicine melts into light and turns into spiritual ambrosia. Dr Yeshi Donden recounted that 'In Tibet there were many people who achieved success in this practice; despite being old, they became young again, living as long as a hundred and thirty or a hundred and fifty years.'

Rituals of attainment

above

Holding the arrow of long life, a Tantric yogin engages in the rites of rejuvenation.

Transforming the cells

opposite

The thangka illustrating the greater elixir of rejuvenation reveals aging as being rooted in physical and mental stress. To reverse this process, essence-elixirs are made from rhododendron flowers, juniper seeds, tansy and ephedra. 'The result will be the attainment of a body with the attributes of a 16-year-old youth, with the prowess of a snow lion, the strength of an elephant, the complexion of a peacock, the speed of a well-trained horse and a life span comparable to that of the sun and moon.'

Alchemy of awareness

left

In order to attain the supreme elixir . . . the highest pinnacle of the Tantric path . . . Cut through to the roots of Mind's inner radiance . . . '

Supreme Nectar-Elixir Dialogue

In the Tibetan medical tradition, techniques for promoting virility are used to restore and enhance sexual performance as well as to increase physical strength and promote longevity. The principal ingredient used in aphrodisiac medicines is the flesh of the white snow frog mixed with various tonifying herbs. Tibetan doctors distinguish between the simple restoration of fertility and the greater objective of enhancing spiritual experience. According to Dr Yeshi Donden, 'The highest purpose of virilification is to enhance the experience of the bliss of union so that the bliss consciousness can be used to realize . . . the emptiness of inherent existence in a totally non-dualistic and powerful way.'

Merits of sensuality

above

To restore sexual potency the medical Tantras prescribe finding 'desirable surroundings with the sweet . . . sound of chirping birds . . . and a beautiful young girl friend . . . Conduct should include . . . pleasant conversation, along with kissing and embracing . . . and aphrodisiac foods.'

Occasions for abstinence

opposite

'One should avoid intercourse with women who are pregnant, weak or emaciated, or whose menstrual fluid is indicative of disorders of Wind, Bile or Phlegm.'

In Tibetan Buddhism the radiant plumage of the peacock is attributed to a diet of poisonous plants, symbolizing the Tantric path which transforms distractive passions into potent energies and heightened awareness. As the Hevajra Tantra proclaims, 'By the very forces whereby others are ensnared, the Tantric gains supreme liberation.'

The fires of liberation

left

'Our nectars merged as a single
 elixir . . .
Self and other dissolving in radiant
 awareness . . .
Innate bliss arising as the utter
 openness of the Great Expanse . . .
Look into the intrinsic freshness of
 your desire and there is boundless
 light.'

The dakini Yeshe Tsogyal

Alchemy of bliss

below

Sexual union arouses all the body's
senses and inner elements, activating
the 'solar' and 'lunar' energies
that flow through the body's inner
mandala. As the mahasiddha
Tilopa proclaimed in his Song of
Mahamudra, 'If you seek a consort,
the wisdom of the union of joy and
emptiness will arise within . . . You
will gain long life, without white
hairs . . . You will wax like the
moon . . . become radiant, and
your strength will be perfect.'

In the path of inner Tantra, desire is not rejected, but used as a
force of transformation, burning through the habitual obscurations
and states of inner contraction that separate us from our innermost
Buddha Nature. Lama Yeshe explained, 'A consort is necessary for
bringing all the pervading energy winds into the central channel . . .
opening the heart centre completely and
experiencing the profoundest levels of
clear light.' In Tantric theory, semen
and its female equivalent are the
body's innate awakening force
(*bodhicitta*) which, retained and
spread through the cells, generates
the bliss used for penetrating to the
luminous core of reality itself.

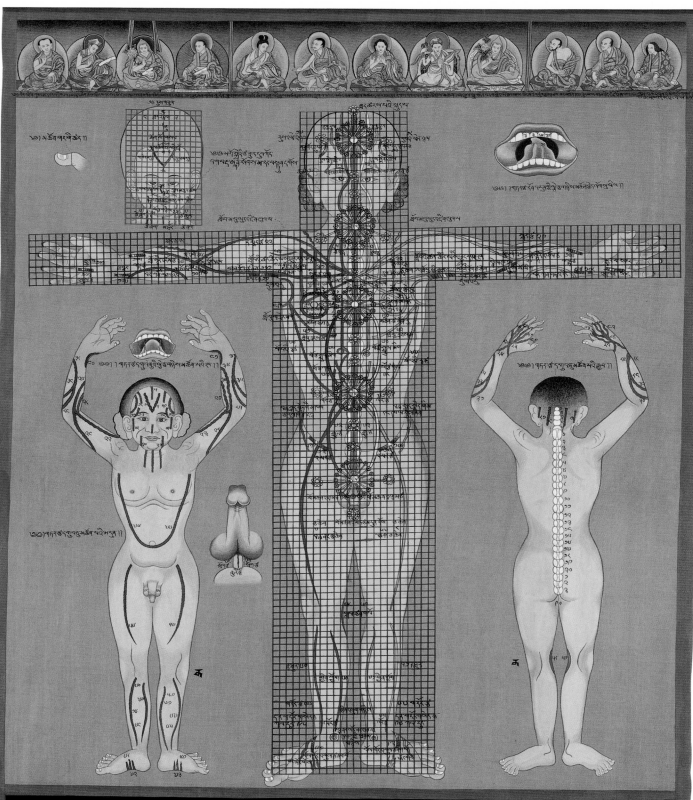

To generate the bliss used in the practices of the inner Tantras, Tibetans also rely on the 'inner wisdom consort' and the male and female polarities within the subtle body. In one of his songs of realization, the great eleventh-century Tibetan yogi Milarepa described the process by which the 'red' and 'white' essences acquired at birth are used to reveal the inseparability of bliss and luminosity:

> 'Bliss arises when the inner fire (*tummo*) blazes
> throughout the body,
> There is bliss when the winds of Roma and Kyangma
> enter into the central channel.
> There is bliss when the *bodhicitta* descends from above
> . . . and the translucent *tigle* pervades from below.
> When the male and female essences unite at the
> heart . . .
> The whole body is suffused with undefiled rapture.
> Sixfold is the bliss of the secret yogas.'

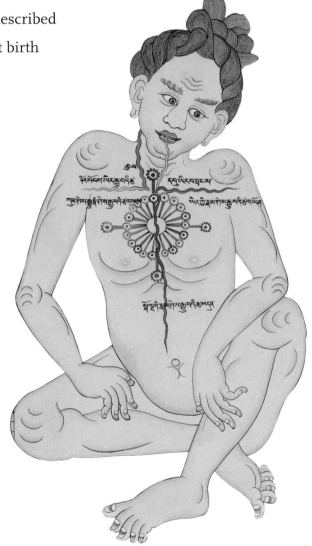

The inner mandala

opposite

The physical body's inner mandala of subtle essences and energy currents is used in Tantric practice as the basis for spiritual transformation.

Anatomy of light

right

'The great Pristine Awareness abides within the body . . . but is not born of the body.'
Hevajra Tantra

Dakinis

above

Portrayed as nymph-like spirits dancing through the sky, dakinis embody the openness and play of the awakening mind.

'Dakinis dance blissfully in the body's psychic veins and secret drops; Mundane perception dissolves And all emanations become radiantly pure . . .'

'Essence of All-Beneficial Ambrosia'

Mandala of Amitayus

left

From his heart chakra radiating healing lights of the five elements, the Buddha of Boundless Life is the ultimate expression of our own innermost nature – an image of wholeness and totality.

Dzogchen channels

right

The body's subtlemost energy channel arises from the heart like a lotus flower emerging from the mire of human conceptions. The *katika* channel is described as a crystal-like tube rising through the upper cavities of the body and emerging at the eyes. The heart energy purified of all defilement radiates its own inner light. As stated in a Tantric text, 'for the person who meditates upon the luminous unchanging sphere that abides for ever within the heart . . .Enlightenment will definitely dawn.'

The Tibetan art of healing leads through the labyrinths of human embodiment to reveal at the core of our physical being the perfectibility of the human spirit. The bliss that arises through the yogas of the inner winds and psychic channels restores wholeness to body, mind and spirit. Unfolding from the lotus of the heart, the body's subtlemost energies reveal the pristine awareness that liberates from all suffering. True healing begins with envisaging a state of perfect health, as enlightenment depends on unshakable faith in the wisdom and luminosity of our innermost nature. The paintings from the Tibetan medical Tantras draw us into a magical realm of compassion and creativity. As the Blue Beryl suggests, if we remain open to their healing influences, all afflictions and delusive emotions can be ultimately liberated in the great expanse of all-pervading light.

Detail of a thangka devoted to aspects of urine
analysis (see p. 106).

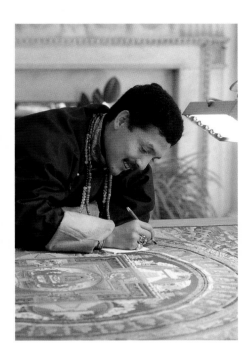

Artist's and Author's Postscripts and Acknowledgments

The artist's role in Tibetan Buddhist culture is to reveal the hidden potential in all human beings. The eyes are the gateway to the innermost spirit, and through them we can experience directly what the mind, otherwise, can only dimly imagine. The images and energy of Tibetan art awaken us to a world of infinite possibility.

All the colours used in my work come from natural sources. The blue is from ground lapis lazuli, the red from cinnabar, the yellow from sulphur salt, combined with the dust of pure gold. Through colours and shapes I try to create worlds in which the simple sense of sight can free us from static images of who and what we are, and what we can become. From my perspective the paintings illustrating the Tibetan medical Tantras are not only visual records of an extraordinary system of knowledge, but in themselves powerful images which stimulate the mind's innate creativity and healing energies.

The healing power of Tibetan art originated in ancient times when access to doctors or medicines was very limited. Vitality was often restored through magical rites, including the unfolding of painted scrolls invested with the power to liberate on sight. Through the eyes the mind was restored to a state of wholeness and the body returned to its natural state of harmony and balance.

The present series of Tibetan medical paintings was created in the hope of spreading healing energy to a modern world through a traditional art form little known in Western countries. In a humble way, with the help of colours, shapes and symbols, I try to express the deep interconnectedness of body, mind and spirit. Sickness flourishes only when we lose our inner sense of balance and when our minds fall victim to the poisons of pride, ignorance, fear and frustration. Among the many messages that I hope to convey in my work, one of the most important is to encourage all human beings to believe in themselves and in their power to awaken the divine in all that they meet. Only then can the vision of one's true potential fully emerge. Through my paintings – through the pathways of vision and light – I try to radiate the energy of healing and joy and to share my conviction that, in this very lifetime, enlightenment is more than just a possibility.

There are many whom I would like to thank for their help and support:Kishor Shrestha and my beloved family; my darling wife Sophie; David and Sally Shaw-Smith; Gareth Onorach a Brun; Gordon and Julie Campbell; Markus O. Speidel; Morrough and Katherine Kavanagh; Ciaran MacGonigal, Royal Hibernian Academy, Gallagher Gallery, Dublin; John Guy and John Clarke, Victoria and Albert Museum, London; Cyril McKeon, Friends of the National Collections of Ireland, Dublin; Robert Knox and Richard Blurton, Department of Oriental Antiquities, British Museum, London; Barbara Dawson and Christine Kennedy, Hugh Lane Municipal Gallery of Modern Art, Dublin; John Hutchinson, Douglas Hyde Gallery, Dublin; Dr Michael Ryan and Jan Chapman, Chester Beatty Library, Dublin; Herr Martin Brauen, Völkerkundemuseum der Universität Zürich; Laila Williamson, American Museum of Natural History, New York; Terese Bartholomew, Asian Art Museum, San Francisco; Mile C. Beach, Freer Gallery of Art, Smithsonian Institution, Washington DC; Dr Praditya Pal, Los Angeles County Museum of Art; Dr Valerie Reynolds, Newark Museum, New Jersey; Dr Joseph M. Dye III, Virginia Museum of Fine Arts, Richmond, VA; Noreen O'Hara, Omeau Baths, Belfast; Anthony Aris, Serindia Publications; Tony and Mary Forte; Lesly Shepard; Stewart Wild, Cecilia Chancellor and Jonathan Rhys-Meyers, whom everybody loves.

Romio Shrestha

The last several years have seen the appearance of detailed, authoritative translations of sections of the Four Medical Tantras (Gyushi) as well as Sangye Gyamtso's commentary, the Blue Beryl (Vaidurya Ngonpo). A two-volume edition of the set of medical paintings preserved in Ulan-Ude was published in 1992 by Serindia Publications and Harry N. Abrams, Inc., along with a translation of the accompanying Tibetan text. These works are of enormous importance to Tibetologists, as well as to students and practitioners of oriental medicine. This current volume is enormously indebted to the authors and translators of these works and in no way aspires to rival their academic initiatives. The approach adopted in this book is not intended so much for the benefit of scholars but to inform those interested in relating the fundamental principles of Tibetan medicine to everyday life – foremost among them being the role of creativity and compassion in initiating the process of healing, both in oneself and in others. The book seeks to fulfil the wish of His Holiness the Dalai Lama that the medical Tantras be made available to a wider audience.

For the purposes of making the vast content of the medical paintings more accessible, individual thangkas and details that best exemplify the Tibetan Buddhist approach to physical, emotional and spiritual well-being have been selected. The text and captions draw on a variety of sources, both published and unpublished, including interviews and discussions with Tibetan lamas and physicians. In the same way that the paintings illustrating the Blue Beryl transform an esoteric body of knowledge into one that is visceral and immediate, the text of the present work seeks to present the paintings in a manner which is equally accessible and illuminating.

There are many who have contributed to making this book a reality. Foremost, I am indebted to His Holiness the Dalai Lama for his encouragement in this attempt to make the philosophy and practice of Tibetan medicine accessible to a wider public, and to the many lamas, yogis and physicians who shared their vision and expertise. I am also enormously indebted to Fernand Meyer, Gyurme Dorje, and the late Yuri Parfionovitch, who painstakingly translated and published the textual inscriptions on the Tibetan medical paintings. I am also immensely grateful to Gordon Campbell, whose commitment and dedication to Romio Shrestha's work first conceived of the possibility of presenting these paintings in book form, and to Romio himself for his inspired vision of 'healing through sight'. My most profound thanks, however, must go to the lineage of Tibetan healers, too numerous to mention individually, who have continuously pointed out that all healing, as all transformation, begins with awareness of the infinite potential of this magical vehicle: the human body/mind.

It is my profound hope that this book may function as a guide for those in good health to make the best use of their physical and mental resources and, at the same time, serve as an inspiration for those who are sick to learn, as Tibetans are taught, the profound lessons which every illness encodes.

Ian Baker

Bibliography

Ambrosia Heart Tantra, The: The secret Oral Teaching on the Eight Branches of the Science of Healing (with annotations by Dr Yeshi Donden; trans. Jhampa Kelsang). Dharamsala: LTWA, 1977

Avedon, John. *In Exile from the Land of Snows*. London: Michael Joseph Ltd, 1984

Beckwith, Christopher I. 'The Introduction of Greek Medicine into Tibet in the Seventh and Eighth Centuries', *Journal of the American Oriental Society* 99 (1979), pp. 297–313

Birnbaum, Raoul. *The Healing Buddha*. Boston, MA: Shambala, 1989

Chang, Garma C. C. *Teachings of Tibetan Yoga*. New York: Carol Publishing Group, 1963

Chopel, Gedun. *Tibetan Arts of Love* (introduced and translated by Jeffrey Hopkins). Ithaca, N.Y.: Snow Lion Publications, 1992

Clifford, Terry. *Tibetan Buddhist Medicine and Psychiatry: The Diamond Healing*. York Beach, ME: Samuel Weiser, 1984

Cozort, Daniel. *Highest Yoga Tantra*. Ithaca, N.Y.: Snow Lion Publications, 1986

Crystal Cave: A Compendium of Teachings by Masters of the Practice Lineage (trans. Erik Pema Kunsang; ed. Ward Brisick). Hong Kong and Kathmandu: Rangjung Yeshe Publications, 1990

Dash, Vaidya Bhagwan. *Tibetan Medicine with Special Reference to Yoga Sataka*. Dharamsala: Library of Tibetan Works and Archives, 1976;

——, *Pharmacopoeia of Tibetan Medicine*. Delhi: Sri Satguru Publications, 1994

Dharmarakshita. *The Wheel of Sharp Weapons* (trans. Geshe Ngawang Dhargyey, Sharpa Tulku, Khamlung Tulku, Alexander Berzin and Jonathan Landaw). Dharamsala: Library of Tibetan Works and Archives, 1976

Donden, Yeshi. *Health Through Balance: An Introduction to Tibetan Medicine*. Ithaca, N.Y.: Snow Lion Publications, 1986

Dudjom Rinpoche, Jikdrel Yeshe Dorje. *The Nyingmapa School of Tibetan Buddhism: Its Fundamentals and History* (trans. and ed. Gyurme Dorje and Matthew Kapstein). Boston, MA: Wisdom Publications, 1991

Dummer, Tom. *Tibetan Medicine and Other Holistic Health-Care Systems*. London: Routledge, 1988

Finckh, Elisabeth. *Studies in Tibetan Medicine*. Ithaca, N.Y.: Snow Lion Publications, 1988

Fundamentals of Tibetan Medicine according to the Rgyud-bzhi. Dharamsala: Tibetan Medical Center, 1981

Guenther, Herbert V. *The Life and Teachings of Naropa*. London: Oxford University Press, 1963

Gyaltsen, Khenpo Konchog, *In Search of the Stainless Ambrosia*. Ithaca, N.Y.: Snow Lion Publications, 1988

Gyatso, Geshe Kelsang. *Clear Light of Bliss: Mahamudra in Vajrayana Buddhism*. London: Wisdom Publications, 1982

Gyatso, Tenzin, H.H. the XIV Dalai Lama. *Freedom in Exile: The Autobiography of the Dalai Lama of Tibet* (edited by John Curtis). London: Hodder & Stoughton, 1990

Gyatso, Tenzin, the Dalai Lama, *Kindness, Clarity, and Insight*. Ithaca, N.Y.: Snow Lion Publications, 1984

Khangkar, Dr Lobsang Dolma *Lectures on Tibetan Medicine* (edited by K. Dhondup). Dharamsala: Library of Tibetan Works and Archives, 1986

Khangkar, Dr Tsewang Dolkar. *Journey into the Mystery of Tibetan Medicine*. Delhi: Yarlung Publications, 1990

Landaw, Jonathan and Andy Weber. *Images of Enlightenment: Tibetan Art in Practice*. Ithaca, N.Y.: Snow Lion Publications, 1993

Lingpa, Rigdzin Jigme. *The Dzogchen Innermost Essence Preliminary Practice* (trans. Tulku Thondrup; ed. Brian Beresford). Delhi and Dharamsala: Library of Tibetan Works and Archives, 1982;

——, 'The Seal of Wisdom Essence: The Most Secret Way to Accomplish the Lama from the Heart Essence of the Vast Expanse' (trans. David Christiansen). Kathmandu, 1987

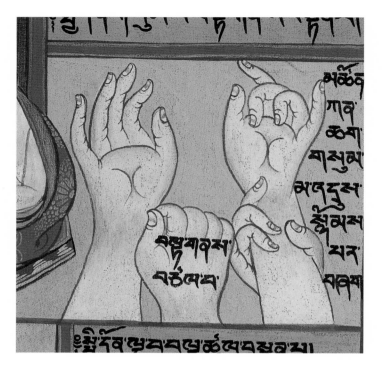

Manjusrimitra. *Primordial Experience: An Introduction to Dzogchen Meditation* (trans. from the Tibetan by Namkhai Norbu and Kennard Lipman). Boston, MA, and London: Shambala Publications, 1986

Mind and Mental Health in Tibetan Medicine. New York: Potala Publications, 1988

Mullin, Glenn H. *Selected Works of the Dalai Lama VII.* Ithaca, N.Y.: Snow Lion Publications, 1982;

——, *The Practice of Kalachakra.* Ithaca, N.Y.: Snow Lion Publications, 1991

Norbu, Namkhai. 'The Mirror of the Luminous Mind'. Rome, 1983;

——, *The Cycle of Day and Night* (edited by John M. Reynolds). Berkeley, CA: Zhang Zhung Editions, 1984;

——, *Dream Yoga and the Practice of Natural Light.* Ithaca, N.Y.: Snow Lion Publications, 1992

Norbu, Thinley. *Magic Dance: The Display of the Self Nature of the Five Wisdom Dakinis.* Paris: Sedag, 1981

Nyima, Chokyi. *The Union of Mahamudra and Dzogchen* (trans. from the Tibetan by Erik Pema Kunsang; edited by Marcia B. Schmidt). Hong Kong and Kathmandu: Rangjung Yeshe Publications, 1986

Pal, Pratapaditya. *Art of Tibet.* Berkeley, CA, and London: University of California Press and Los Angeles County Museum of Art, 1983;

——, *Tibetan Paintings: A Study of Tibetan Thangkas Eleventh to Nineteenth Centuries.* Paris, New York, Hong Kong: Ravi Kumar, Publisher, 1988

Parfionovitch, Yuri, Gyurme Dorje, Fernand Meyer. *Tibetan Medical Paintings, Illustrations to the Blue Beryl Treatise of Sangye Gyamtso (1653–1705),* 2 vols., London: Serindia Publications, 1992

Quintessence Tantras of Tibetan Medicine, The (trans. Dr Barry Clark). Ithaca, N.Y.: Snow Lion Publications, 1995

Rapgay, Dr Lobsang. *Tibetan Medicine: A Holistic Approach to Better Health.* Dharamsala: private publication, 1985;

——, *Tibetan Therapeutic Massage.* Dharamsala: private publication, 1985

Sangpo, Khetsun. *Tantric Practice in Nyingmapa* (trans. and ed. Jeffrey Hopkins). Ithaca, N.Y.: Gabriel/Snowlion, 1982

Shabkar, Lama, Jatang Tsogdruk Rangdrol. *Flight of the Garuda* (trans. Erik Pema Kunsang). Hong Kong and Kathmandu: Rangjung Yeshe Publications, 1986

Shantideva. *A Guide to the Bodhisattva's Way of Life* (trans. Stephen Batchelor). Dharamsala: Library of Tibetan Works and Archives, 1979

Snellgrove, David L. and Hugh E. Richardson. *A Cultural History of Tibet.* Boulder, CO: Prajna Press, 1968

Sogyal Rinpoche. *The Tibetan Book of Living and Dying.* San Francisco, CA: HarperCollins, 1992

Stein, R.A., *Tibetan Civilization.* London: Faber and Faber, 1972

Svoboda, Robert and Arnie Lade, *Tao and Dharma: Chinese Medicine and Ayurveda.* Twin Lakes, WI: Lotus Press, 1995

Thondrup, Tulku. *Buddha Mind: An Anthology of Longchen Rabjam's Writings of Dzogpa Chenpo* (ed. Harold Talbott). Ithaca, N.Y.: Snow Lion Publications, 1989;

——, *The Healing Power of Mind.* Boston, MA: Shambala Publications, 1996

Thurman, Robert A.F. and Marilyn M. Rhie. *Wisdom and Compassion: The Sacred Art of Tibet.* New York: Harry N. Abrams, 1991

Trungpa, Chogyam. *Cutting through Spiritual Materialism.* Berkeley, CA: Shambala Publications, 1973;

——, *The Heart of the Buddha.* Boston, MA, and London: Shambala Publications, 1991

Tsarong, T.J. *Handbook of Traditional Tibetan Drugs.* Kalimpong, India: Tibetan Medical Publications, 1986;

——, *Tibetan Medical Plants.* Kalimpong, India: Tibetan Medical Publications, 1994

Urgyen, Tulku. *Vajra Heart.* Kathmandu: Rangjung Yeshe Publications, 1988

Van Alphen, Jan and Anthony Aris (eds.). *Oriental Medicine: an Illustrated Guide to the Asian Arts of Healing.* London: Serindia Publications, 1995

Yeshe, Lama Thubten. *Introduction to Tantra: A Vision of Totality.* Boston, MA, and London: Wisdom Publications, 1987

Tibetan medical resources

Tibet

Tibetan Medical Institute
(Mentsikhang)
Lhasa
Tel.: 86-891 6323231

India and Nepal

Men-Tsee-Khang (Tibetan Medical
and Astrological Institute)
Gangchen Kyishong
Dharamsala-176215
Distt. Kangra (H.P.)
Tel.: 91-1892 22618
Fax: 91-1892 24116
e-mail: tmai@dsala.tibet.net

Dr Yeshi Donden
'Ashok NIwas'
McLeod Ganj
Dharamsala-176215
Distt. Kangra (H.P.)

Dr Trogawa Rinpoche
Chakpori Medical Institute
P.O. North Point
Darjeeling-734104
West Bengal
Tel./fax: 91-354 53016

Dr Tsewang Dolkar Khangkar
Dolkar House
D-10, Kalkaji
New Delhi-110019
Tel.: 91-11 642 9863/ 646 5240

Dr Kunsang Dorje
Kunphen Tibetan Medical Centre
P.O. Box 3428
Chetrapati, Kathmandu
Tel.: 977-1 251920

Dr Tsering Choekyi
Kailash Medical Institute
Maijubahal Chabahil
P.O. Box 2823
Kathmandu
Tel.: 977-1 474025

Lhamo Dolkar – Spirit Medium
c/o Thargay lama
G.P.O. Box 4170
Boudhanath, Kathmandu

United Kingdom

Dr Tamdin Bradley
122 Northcote Road
London E17 7EB
Tel.: 0181-521 4681

Kate Roddick
Life Centre
15 Edge Street
London W8 7PN
Tel.: 0171-221 4602

The Tara College of Tibetan Medicine
250 Ferry Road
Edinburgh EH5 3AM
Tel./ Fax: 0131-552 1431

Samye Ling Tibetan Centre
Eskdalemuir
Dumfriesshire DG13 OQL
Tel.: 01387 373232
Fax: 01387 373223

United States of America

Chakpori Foundation
Dr Shakya Dorje
Eliot Trokar
151–31 88th Street, Box 2D
Howard Beach, N.Y. 11414
(1) 718-641 7323
e-mail: etokar@aol.com

Dr Philip Weber, M.D.
Boulder, CO
(1) 303-449 5774

Dr Diki Paldon Narongshar
San Francisco, CA
(1) 415-776 9531

'To cure the essence of illness don't take even a single dose of medicine or chant one syllable of a healing ceremony. Don't regard the illness as a hindrance, or consider it a virtue. Leave your mind unfabricated and free . . . Cutting through the flow of conceptual thoughts . . . old illnesses will disappear by themselves and you will remain unharmed by new ones.'

Padmasambhava, eighth-century Tantric master